Performance of Integrated Milk Co-operatives

CMA Monograph Series No. 111

PERFORMANCE OF INTEGRATED MILK CO-OPERATIVES

(A study of Selected Co-operative Dairies in Gujarat and Maharashtra)

C.G. Ranade
D.P. Mathur
B. Rangarajan
V.K. Gupta

INDIAN INSTITUTE OF MANAGEMENT, AHMEDABAD

AND

CONCEPT PUBLISHING COMPANY, NEW DELHI 110059

ISBN-81-7022-033-5

First Published 1988

Published by
Ashok Kumar Mittal
Concept Publishing Company
A/15-16, Commercial Block, Mohan Garden
NEW DELHI-110059

Photocomposed at
Microtech Advance Printing Systems (P) Ltd.
NEW DELHI-110059

Printed at
Taj Press
A-35/4, Maya Puri
NEW DELHI

FOREWORD

Cooperative organizations have been promoted in the developing countries as an instrument of social change and development. In India cooperatives have a long history. From the Second Five Year Plan onwards efforts were made to link credit with marketing. Lately, it has been realized that marketing encompassing all operations, including transportation, handling, drying, processing, storage and warehousing, are critical for the improvement in the socio-economic status of the small farmers. Not only should the small farmers have the benefit of modern technology and management but that these must be under his control and ownership. Following it, the Government has encouraged commodity cooperatives in the country which have attempted backward, forward and horizontal integration. Such cooperatives now exist for sugar, milk, oilseeds, cotton and other commodities.

The authors of the study hypothesized that such cooperatives as develop backward, forward and horizontal integration are able to increase the income of the small farmers through rationalization of costs and through undertaking value addition functions. The study explores this hypothesis and concludes that such cooperatives in the milk industry have indeed played an important role. Not only have they assisted the small farmer in increasing his income from their milk operations substantially but they also have helped landless labourers to undertake milk production as a primary occupation. The authors emphasize the fact that, in the case of milk, the cooperatives have become strong farmers' organizations and have functioned more effectively when fully integrated.

I am sure the study will be useful to policy-makers as well as to managers in understanding the major thrust for action in the rural development programmes in general and in the development of agro-industries programmes in particular.

Centre for Management in Agriculture
Indian Institute of Management
Ahmedabad
December 1, 1985

Ranjit Gupta
Chairman

ACKNOWLEDGMENTS

This monograph is the outcome of a project which the Centre for Management in Agriculture (CMA) had undertaken with financial support from the Ministry of Agriculture, Government of India. We are grateful to the Ministry for their support.

In undertaking this study we had received valuable help from executives of the dairy unions both in Gujarat and Maharashtra. In particular, we would like to thank: B. K. Rabari, Managing Director, Sabarkantha District Cooperative Milk Producers' Union Limited; B. C. Bhatt, Managing Director, Mehsana District Cooperative Milk Producers' Union Limited; H. A. Ghasia, Manager (Animal Husbandry), Surat District Cooperative Milk Producers' Union Limited; C. N. Gulve, Managing Director, Warananagar Cooperative Milk Producers' Union Limited; A. M. Shinde, Manager Krishnakore Cooperative Milk Producers' Union Limited; and G. S. Sankpal, Manager, Hanuman Cooperative Milk Producers' Union Limited.

We would also like to thank Professors A. D. Shinde, P. S. Rao, and V. M. Hilage of Chh. Sahu Central Institute of Business Education and Research, Kolhapur, for introducing us to the dairy officials of Kolhapur and Sangli districts as well as extending assistance during field work.

We are also grateful to the village officials of the Cooperative milk societies as well as farmers of the selected areas for their kind cooperation and hospitality during our field work.

We are indebted to Professors D. K. Desai and U. K. Srivastava of the Indian Institute of Management, Ahmedabad, for their valuable comments and suggestions. During our entire period of study Dr. C. Gopinath, ex-Chairman, and Prof. Ranjit Gupta, present Chairman, CMA, Dr. I. G. Patel, ex-Director, and Dr. N. R. Sheth, present Director, IIMA, have been a constant source of encouragement.

We wish to express special thanks to Mr. Janardhana Rao for his secretarial assistance.

It is needless to add that all observations and conclusions are our own and for any shortcomings, we alone are responsible.

CGR
DPM
BR
VKG

CONTENTS

LIST OF TABLES

LIST OF EXHIBITS

FIGURES

ONE

INTRODUCTION

The economic and social conditions prevailing in rural India in the beginning of the century had led the then policy-makers to believe that a cooperative institutional framework could be conducive for the transformation of the traditional society and pave the way for modernization of agriculture. The subsequent growth of cooperatives was in conformity with this thinking. The strategy at that stage, however, centred around replacement of private credit by institutional credit. It was only after independence and particularly during the Second Five Year Plan period that the linkage between agricultural production, credit, marketing,and processing began to be considered. The assumption was that, to provide to small farmers remunerative prices for their agricultural produce, cooperatives need to undertake marketing and processing activities. Non-credit cooperatives were organized to undertake production, marketing and processing of agricultural and livestock products.

The phenomenal increase in non-credit cooperatives[1] is evident from the fact that in 1977-78 there were 156,817 such societies with a membership of about 24 million. In order to handle these activities, non-credit cooperatives had 925,000 employees. In 1977-78 they had a working capital of Rs. 4,808 crore with a sales turnover of Rs. 3,972 crore (See Table 1.1. for additional information). It is important of note from the table that the sales to working capital ratio is **adverse** in most cases.

---

1. These also include industrial societies not dealing in agricultural produce, consumer stores and housing societies.

1.1 Trends in the Progress of Sectoral Activities

An examination of the progress of selected types of non-credit cooperatives in the First, Second, Third and Fourth Five Year Plan and by the end of 1977-78 (up to which year detailed data are available) shows some distinguishing features. Among the cooperatives handling agricultural farm products, the highest increase was observed for farming societies. In respect of general marketing and other processing societies the progress has been far from satisfactory.

It appears that the objective of large coverage of the population by cooperatives was reasonably fulfilled. Increase in membership was pronounced in the case of sugar cooperatives. Similarly cotton cooperatives also recorded an increase in membership. Relatively, cooperatives performing general marketing functions did not experience increased membership to the level of specialized cooperatives such as sugar mills and cotton processing units. Similarly it was expected that over agricultural processing cooperatives will also have a large coverage but during this period the index reached only 142.

TABLE 1.1 : Important Indicators of Non-Credit Cooperatives in India, 1977-78.

Type of Society	Number (00)	Membership (in lakhs)	Working Capital (Rs. in crores)	Sales Value (Rs. in crores)
1. Marketing	40	59	1299	2202
2. Agricultural processing	10	15	1218	560
3. Farming	97	3	31	7
4. Weavers	144	11	152	109
5. Other Industrial	249	15	91	69
6. Consumers	163	62	187	315
7. All other non-credit	865	75	1830	710*
Total	1568	240	4808	3972

* Excludes Irrigation and Housing Societies for which sales figures are not available.

Source: Statistical Statement of the Cooperative Movement in India, Bombay, Reserve Bank of India, 1979.

A comparative study of per-society membership among different types of non-credit societies raises yet another important issue. Sugar mills had the highest per-society membership of over 5,900 followed by cooperatives handling general marketing functions, cotton ginning and processing and other processing societies. The details of the index of number, membership and per-society membership amongst different categories of non-credit cooperatives in different plan periods are provided in Table 1.2 Data on the number, membership and sales turnover of the above selected type of cooperatives are given in Exhibit 1.1.

Thus it can be observed that the progress in the development of coverage of membership has not been uniform. Among the cooperatives handling agricultural products, those handling sugarcane and cotton processing have done well, cooperatives dealing with other agricultural products not so well. This implies that the advantages accrued only to a limited number of persons involved in the cultivation of these commodities and so warrants a detailed look.

1.2 Cooperative Processing of Agricultural and Livestock Products

Farm business activities in India comprise raising of crops and rearing of livestock usually as a subsidiary occupation. Such behavioural aspect reflects the tendency among the farming communities to meet the food, fodder and nutritional requirements from the farm enterprise alone. The promoters of cooperative movement in the country were aware of this situation and over the period organized cooperative societies to handle farm and livestock products.

However, a significant change in the policy of cooperative development was evident in the Second Five Year Plan period when the role of cooperatives in processing agricultural and livestock products was emphasized to provide a higher value of their produce to the farmers. Cooperatives were organized in the field of marketing and processing of foodgrains, oilseeds, cotton and jute, and cash crops such as sugarcane, fruits, vegetables, coffee, tea, rubber and spices. In the animal husbandry sector, dairy, poultry and fisheries cooperatives were set up. A detailed examination of the agricultural marketing and processing cooperatives reveals four distinguishing

TABLE 1.2 : Important Indicators of Progress of Different Types of Non-Credit Cooperatives in India, 1960-61 to 1977-78.

Type of Coopera-tives	Indicators	By the end of Second Five Year Plan 1960-61	By the end of Third Five Year Plan 1965-66	By the end of Fourth Five Year Plan 1973-74	1977-78
1. General Marketing	1. Index of No. of Societies	100	103	106	116
	2. Index of Membership	100	155	210	239
	3. Membership per Society	472	713	939	977
2. Sugar Mills	1. Index of No. of Societies	100	118	239	282
	2. Index of Membership	100	167	423	621
	3. Membership per Society	2681	3794	4748	5908
3. Farming	1. Index of No. of Societies	100	229	298	304
	2. Index of Membership	100	212	299	395
	3. Membership per Society	28	26	28	34
4. Cotton Ginning & Pressing	1. Index of No. of Societies	100	121	159	178
	2. Index of Membership	100	180	266	360
	3. Membership per Society	461	687	770	927
5. Other Processing	1. Index of No. of Societies	100	61	25	20
	2. Index of Membership	100	163	157	142
	3. Membership per Society	39	104	247	278

Source: Calculated from the data provided in the **statistical statements relating to the Cooperative Movement in India, Part II, Non-Credit Societies,** Reserve Bank of India, Bombay.

features. First, cooperatives were involved in mechanical and manual processing. For instance, cooperatives processed paddy through hand-pounding and mechanical methods in modern rice mills. Second, cooperatives were organized to integrate marketing, processing and utilization of by-products, though commodities thus handled were few. Third, through the pyramidal structure, cooperatives attempted to be broadbased through the primary village societies. Fourth, depending on the activity, primary processing units also attempted to enlarge the coverage of membership. In respect of sugarcane, coverage was large and distinct and membership of such a society has been even to the extent of about 10,000 persons.

1.3 Dynamics of Integrated Cooperative Structure

Conceptually, vertical integration in a commodity system envisages considerable value addition through an increase in agricultural production (productivity), efficient marketing including processing, and fullest possible utilization of by-products so that the producer has increased returns on his labour and land. Since cooperatives' organizational structure was already developed over the years in the country, it was felt that such a structure would be quite conducive to the development of cooperative societies desiring vertical integration, particularly in agricultural commodities, and that such activities would ameliorate the economic conditions of farm producers in particular and village communities in general. Experience has also shown that despite strong ties of farmers with the resident traders who wielded considerable influence in the village, cooperatives developed as a competitive agency.

Since cooperative marketing societies were already in existence, the National Cooperative Development Corporation was established in 1962 to work as the central unit for providing financial and technical assistance in setting up cooperative processing units. Till 1977-78, little over 2,000 processing cooperatives of 30 types had already been established along with over 3,000 specialized marketing societies to undertake the following activities:

(a) to supply farm production requisites such as chemicals, fertilizers, improved seeds, pesticides and agricultural machinery,
(b) to poll and market the farm produce of members,
(c) to undertake processing of farm produce and utilization of by-products for further processing to provide higher value addition, and

(d) to supply consumer articles like sugar, kerosene, controlled cloth, foodgrains, etc., at reasonable prices.

Interestingly, to meet the above objectives, specialized cooperatives both in marketing and processing spheres made significant strides. The value of agricultural inputs distributed through cooperatives increased from Rs.35.7 crore in 1960-61 to Rs.1,499 crore in 1977-78. Similarly, the value of agricultural produce marketed through cooperatives increased from Rs.171 crore in 1960-61 to Rs.1,834 crore in 1977-78. To undertake processing of main and by-products, several other by-product units were established for the processing of rice bran, groundnut oilcake, cotton spinning, cold storages for perishables and manufacturing of paper from rice straw. Also the supply of daily necessities to the rural consumers increased from Rs.22.7 crore in 1961-62 to Rs.624 crore in 1977-78 (Exhibit 1.2).

1.4 Rationale of the Present Study

Despite progress in the organization of cooperatives, coverage of membership and heavy capital investment (to the extent of Rs.179.63 crores in 1977-78), the objectives of integrated cooperative structure to increase value addition function through cooperatives and thus increasing the members' income have been fulfilled only partially. Most specialized marketing and processing societies had no integration between production enhancement efforts (supply of credit and agrochemicals), marketing, processing and by-product utilization.[2] Each cooperative unit mostly worked in a specialized field without entering into close coordination with other cooperatives engaged in related activities of marketing and processing. This situation did not increase the farmer's share in value added, which was possible due to manufacturing of products in different stages. As an instance, the general marketing societies worked in isolation without an active participation in the processing societies located in the same area despite the fact that they were members of the processing society. As a consequence they not only often faced a crisis in procuring the

---

2. Mathur and V.K. Gupta, Management in Cooperative Rice Mills, IIM, Ahmedabad, 1982.

produce of the members in the area of their operation but also could not play the facilitative role of providing agricultural requisites. It may be central observed that out of 4,001 marketing societies (State, Central and primary units) in 1977-78, as many as 36 per cent were not engaged in marketing activity and were dormant. Of the remaining, only 32 per cent were doing business of over Rs. 5 lakh during the year.[3] As against this backdrop, cooperatives were not able to play an effective role in providing agricultural requisites and pooling of the produce for marketing. During the period under review the cooperatives' share in the supply of requisites never exceeded 20 per cent of the total used. Similarly the gross value of agricultural produce marketed by the cooperatives was only 10 per cent of the the national production (Table 1.3). Apart from the above, there were organizational weaknesses. Most of the key personnel in the cooperative structure were deputationists and had little business acumen and motivation.

However, against the above overall dismal picture, there are regional specializations and success stories of specialized commodity cooperatives having a degree of integration and operational efficiency. This is reflected in the higher remunerative prices offered by cooperatives for members' produce and welfare measures undertaken by them. Complete and partial success in achieving integration has been observed in the case of some commodities such as milk, sugarcane and cotton. In the case of these commodities the cooperatives did attempt to develop an organization at the village level, enroll members to participate in their activities of supplying requisites and pooling of the members' produce for marketing and processing, utilization of by-products for further processing, and providing welfare incentives. Again in these efforts there were regional and intra-regional differences. For example, integration in dairying has been most successful in the southern, central and northern parts of Gujarat, and sugarcane commodity has had success in western Maharashtra. Organized cooperatives for some of the above commodities also had organizational strengths by way of engaging the

---

3. Dantwale Committee had recommended business of Rs. 5 lakh per year for economic viability of a cooperative marketing society. This amount was raised to Rs. 20 lakh in 1970.

professional staff of their own and an organizational network in far-off villages to have a continuous flow of the commodity for processing. Such a situation warrants an in-depth study regarding the performance of integrated, particularly output-based, cooperatives to replicate the experiences gained in a geographic region. The present study is an attempt in this direction and is confined to purposively selected dairy cooperatives.

TABLE 1.3 : Share of Cooperatives in Handling Agricultural Produce and Supply of Agricultural Requisites, 1960-61 to 1977-78.

Period	% of agricultural produce handled by cooperatives to the gross value of agricultural production in India	% of agricultural requisites supplied by cooperative to the gross value of agricultural inputs used in India
End of II Plan (1960-61)	10.8	2.8
End of III Plan (1965-66)	1.8	5.6
End of IV Plan	4.7	20.1
1977-78	9.8	15.1

Source: Estimated on the basis of data provided in the **National Accounts Statistics** for the period 1960-61 to 1977-78 and **Statistical Statements Relating to the Cooperative Movement in India, Part II,** 1977-78, Bombay, RBI.

1.5 Dairy Industry in India

According to the latest available statistics, the gross value of output from livestock rearing in India, at current prices, has increased from Rs. 3,197 crores in 1970-71 to Rs. 8,618 crores in 1979-80. Livestock rearing constituted 20 per cent of the total value of output from agriculture and allied activities in 1979-80 at current prices (Table 1.4). At constant prices also, the share of the value of output from livestock formed about 19 per cent of the the total value of output from agriculture and allied activities in 1979-80. However, it is important to mention that the share of output from livestock rearing did not substantially change. Such a situation warrants an in-depth analysis of the impact of livestock rearing enterprise, particularly in meeting the milk requirements of urban and rural areas. However, it is important to note that during the last few years, new technologies have been introduced in the field of milk preservation, processing and marketing of liquid milk, and processed by-products, with the broad objective of providing benefits to producers and consumers.

1.6 Trends in Milk Production and Consumption

According to available data, domestic milk production increased from 17.406 million metric tonnes in 1951 to 34.600 million metric tonnes in 1982-83 (Table 1.5). However, during the period 1950-51 to 1971-72, milk production averaged around 18 million metric tonnes per year and showed a sharp increase later. It appears that this situation was a contributing factor in maintaining the substantial share in the total value of output from agriculture and allied activities in the national income. But the increase in milk production seems to have had no impact in increasing the per capita consumption by the urban and rural population. This was reflected from the fact that the per capita milk consumption has not shown any appreciable increase in the period between 1951-52 and 1982-83. Per capita consumption was 132 grams per day in 1951 and declined to 107 in 1969-70 and the recovery in the later years could surpass the consumption level of 1951 only in 1982-83. This was despite the fact that India imported 43,000 tonnes of milk powder annually between 1960 and 1969 which declined in later years.

1.7 Role of Cooperatives in the Dairy Industry

To develop dairying in India, a national programme was envisaged during the planning exercises with an outlay of Rs. 4,855 million in 1975. Under the programme two national bodies were created to undertake various dairy projects to cover rural families for procurement, processing and marketing under the framework of cooperatives. It seems that the broad objectives of such a programme were to provide an assured market for the rural milk suppliers throughout the year and reducing inter-regional as well as seasonal imbalances of milk production and availability to the urban and rural consumers. With this end in view till 1982-83, over 23,000 village cooperatives were organized in different States in India with over 2.6 million members. To improve the productivity of milch animals the programme of breed improvement was started through

TABLE 1.4 : Share of Gross Value of Output from Livestock to the Gross Value of output from Agriculture and Allied Activities in India, 1970-71 to 1979-80.

(in core Rs.)

Year	Value of Current Prices		Value at constant prices (1970-71 = 100)			
	Total Value of output from Agri-culture & allied activities	Value of output from Livestock	Total Value of output from Agri-culture & allied activities	Index 1970-71 = 100	Value of output from Livestock	Index 1970-71 = 100
1970-71	20729	3197(15.4)	20729	100.0	3197(15.4)	100.0
1973-74	31995	4600(14.4)	21051	101.6	3430(16.3)	107.3
1974-75	35749	5549(15.5)	20832	100.5	3583(17.2)	112.1
1975-76	34175	6147(17.9)	23213	111.9	3839(16.5)	120.0
1976-77	35786	6654(18.6)	22167	106.9	3946(17.8)	123.4
1977-78	40686	7145(17.6)	24630	118.8	4032(16.4)	126.1
1978-79	41227	7789(18.9)	25121	121.1	4115(16.4)	128.7
1979-80	42838	8618(20.1)	22643	109.2	4206(18.6)	131.6

Note: Figures in brackets indicate the share of the value of livestock product to the total value from agriculture and allied activities.

Source: Various issues of **National Accounts Statistics,** Central Statistical Organisation, New Delhi.

TABLE 1.5 : Milk Production and Per Capita Consumption in India, 1951-52 to 1982-83.

Period	Milk Production in the year (Million Metric Tonnes)	Per Capita Milk Consumption (g/day)	Index of per capita milk consumption with 1951 = 100
1951-52	(17.406)	132	100.0
1956-57	(19.717)	135	102.3
1961-62	(20.375)	127	96.2
1966-67	(19.368)	108	81.8
1969-70	(20.740)	107	81.1
1971-72	(22.500)	112	84.4
1977-78	(28.300)	123	93.2
1978-79	(29.110)	124	93.9
1979-80	(30.200)	126	95.5
1980-81	(31.500)	128	97.0
1981-82	(32.900)	131	99.2
1982-83	(34.600)	135	102.3

Source: **Operational Flood: A Reality,**

Indian Dairy Corporation, 1983, Baroda.

the setting up of 3,252, artificial insemination centres throughout the country. Intensive surveys were conducted to find out potential milk surplus areas and 436 veterinary routes were identified for milk collection and to provide veterinary services to milk producers on these routes. The village level cooperative structure was developed to achieve backward and forward integration (Exhibit 1.3). Feeder dairy plants located in the identified milkshed areas provided veterinary facilities, cattlefeed at the reasonable prices from their installed plants, and made arrangements for transportation of milk to the plant site. As a consequence there was a perceptible change in the milk procurement of these feeder dairy plants. According to the available data, milk procurement nearly doubled from 26.73 lakh kg a day in 1980-81 to 50.36 lakh kg a day in 1982-83.

However, the efforts have not yielded uniform results in the flow of marketing of milk throughout the country. The achievements were marked in certain regions and selected pockets. Total milk procurement through the established infrastructural development could mop up only 1.8 million tonnes of milk from the rural areas of the country

TABLE 1.6 : Comparison of Selected Characteristics of the Milk Cooperatives in Gujarat with other Regions in India, 1982-83.

State and Region	Number of village coopera-tives	Member-ship per society	Milk Procurement day (kgs.) per Society	per Member	No. of villages under the jurisdic-tion of AI centres	No. of villages per veterinary route
1. Gujarat	7033	141	295	2.09	11	53
2. Western Region	9187	125	296	2.36	9	51
3. Northern Region	5612	64	145	2.27	9	52
4. Southern Region	7309	145	198	1.37	9	67
5. Eastern Region	1231	39	69	1.77	3	38
6. Union Territories	170	81	131	1.62	-	-
Total	23509	112	217	1.93	8	55

Source: Annual Report 1982-83, National Dairy Development Board, Anand, 1983.

in 1982-83 which was a small fraction of the total milk production and marketed surplus. Further examination of available data indicates that performance of cooperatives in terms of development of infrastructure development was better in the western and southern regions. More than 70 per cent of the village level cooperatives specializing in milk were established in the western and southern regions. About 30 per cent of the village cooperatives in 1982-83 were only in Gujarat. In terms of membership per society the western and southern regions had a relatively higher membership than others (Table 1.6). As compared with Gujarat where the per society membership was 141, in the southern regions it was 145 per society and in other regions membership per society was quite low. Similarly in respect of the programme of improvement in cattle breed each artificial insemination centre covered about nine villages in the western, southern and northern regions. To facilitate milk procurement from the villages, each veterinary route covered about 50 villages in the western and northern regions while the southern region covered more than 65 villages.

The eastern region had the lowest number of villages per veterinary route. The quantity of milk procured per society and per member was the highest in both cases in the western region. Perday milk procurement was 296 kg per society in the western region and 198 kg per society in the southern region. In other regions it was quite low. Higher perday milk procurement per society in Gujarat is the distinguishing feature of the western region. In the southern region, despite the highest membership per society, per-member milk procurement per day was the lowest (1.37 kg).

1.8 Objectives

The specific objectives of the present study are:

(i) to examine structural characteristics of different segments of the milk commodity cooperative system (production, marketing and processing),

(ii) to study the functional aspects of backward and forward linkages and evaluate the performance of various sub-systems,

(iii) to estimate the direct and indirect economic and social benefits due to vertical integration to the members of the cooperatives, and

(iv) to suggest ways and means to improve the operational efficiency of various sub-systems in the integrated cooperatives and increase producers' share in the consumer rupee, especially in other areas where such cooperatives have not achieved comparable results.

1.9 Methodological Approach

1.9.1 Selection of Region

As already mentioned there are two State level federations, 167 union and 20,703 primary societies engaged in milk commodity throughout the country. In terms of the relative position of coverage of villages, membership and value of milk purchased, both Gujarat and Maharashtra are the leading (Exhibit 1.4) states in India. About 22 per cent and 24 per cent of the primary societies in India are located in Gujarat and Maharashtra respectively. Similarly 10 per cent of the unions are located in Gujarat and 43 per cent in Maharashtra. However, the degree of vertical integration is considerably different between the two States. The Gujarat cooperative dairies mostly have composite milk plants and manufacture several products other than supplying liquid milk to urban milk distribution schemes. Maharashtra, on the other hand, has cooperative dairies which usually function as liquid milk suppliers to the Bombay Milk Scheme and others. Keeping in view the objectives of the study, Gujarat and Maharashtra were for the study. It needs to be noted that the dairy cooperatives in Gujarat are relatively older.

1.9.2 Selection of Districts/Dairy Plants

In Gujarat, 14 districts have village cooperatives dealing in milk and plants for fuller utilization of milk and by-products. Since several studies have been undertaken on milk producers of Kaira district, the district was excluded from our study. On the basis of ranks of village cooperatives in the area of operation, membership per society and perday milk procurement, three districts having dairy processing plants and structural facilities for the development of milch cattle population were selected (Exhibit 1.5). These were:

Mehsansa District Milk producers' Union (1962), Sabarkantha District Milk Producers' Union (1967) and Surat District Milk producers' Union (1951).[4]

As stated earlier dairy development in Maharashtra has yet to keep pace with that in Gujarat. Moreover, they were structured on a different pattern. In Gujarat Union were established at district level while in Maharashtra there was more then one union in the district and these had a smaller jurisdiction than in Gujarat. Two unions were selected in Kolhapur. Both these unions, namely, Yalguda (1970) and Warananagar, were selected because they had different organizational structures. In addition, a union in the adjoining district of Sangli, namely, Miraj Union (1970), was also selected. The rationale behind the approach followed in Maharashtra was to examine variations in milk procurement, processing and distribution of milk. These unions were established primarily to serve as feeder units for Bombay. In many ways these unions were not fully integrated dairies because they had neither freedom to manufacture products nor freedom in respect of price nor in respect of place to sell liquid milk. Thus vertical integration was only partial. Similarly, none of these unions had a cattlefeed plant or extensive veterinary services. In this manner backward integration was also not complete. In a sense Maharashtra would serve as a control area for comparison with Gujarat.

1.9.3 Selection of Villages

Since our objective was to understand advantages of integrated cooperatives to small farmers, it was necessary to select villages and farmers. Each selected dairy unit had a well-designed system to procure milk from the villages. Each unit had milk collection routes. Five major routes supplying milk to the dairy were identified. From these five routes, five villages were selected on the basis of highest per member milk supply in the 1980-81 season on the route to the dairy unit. Thus, for three dairy units, 15 villages were selected in Gujarat and a same number in Maharashtra.

---

4. Figures in brackets indicate the year of establishment.

1.9.4 Selection of Farmers

For each of the selected village, a list was prepared of the dairy farmers supplying milk to the dairy plant and the farmers were classified into three categories:

(i) Small: farmers supplying less than five litres per day,
(ii) Medium: farmers supplying between five and 10 litres per day,
(iii) Big: farmers supplying more than 10 litres per day.

Besides the above categories, an attempt was made to identify non-members in each of the above categories who were not selling milk to the cooperative dairy plant to have comparative performance of members and non-members of cooperatives. Non-members were thus an additional control point within each State for estimation of benefits of integration. The distribution of sample dairy farmers in Gujarat and Maharashtra is provided in Exhibit 1.6. It is important to note that the selection of member farmers in small, medium and big categories was in proportion to the total number of suppliers in the selected villages.

Originally, we had planned for 300 milk producers as the sample size for our study,out of which 225 were to be members and 75 non-members of the dairy cooperatives in each state, Gujarat and Maharashtra. However, when the sample was actually drawn from selected villages, we could retain the same number of members, but for the non-members only 31 milk producers in Gujarat and 43 milk producers in Maharashtra could be selected for the study (Exhibit 1.6). Because some members did not have a single household which was not a member of the dairy cooperative, their sample size had to be reduced. This reduction in the sample size was compensated for by an increase in the sample size for the members of dairy cooperatives.

Comparing the distribution of members and non-members across the size class, it is evident that the percentage of small non-member producers is the highest. In Gujarat out of 31 most of the non-members are small, while there are 33 out of 43 small non-member in Maharashtra. This is the result of two factors. First, in the Indian villages the number of small producers is usually 10 times that of big producers. Second, some small producers have so little and uncertain a marketable surplus of milk that they are not net suppliers of milk, and hence do not become members of the dairy cooperatives.

1.10 Period of Study

Data collected from the sample dairy farmers refer to the period between July 1981 and June 1982. For the analysis of the data of the selected dairy unions, preceding five years between 1976-77 and 1981-82 were considered.

Exhibit 1.1. : Progress of Selected Types of Primary Non-Credit Societies, 1960-61 to 1977-78.

Particulars	Year	Marketing	Agricultural Processing	Farming
1. Number	1960-61	3108	3297	3184
	1965-66	3198	2127	7295
	1973-74	3278	1129	9477
	1977-78	3592	1034	9697
2. Membership ('000)	1960-61	1468	356	82
	1965-66	2280	600	188
	1973-74	3077	1097	264
	1977-78	3510	1484	325
3. Sales (Rs. in crores)	1960-61	106	42	2
	1965-66	317	110	4
	1973-74	692	447	10
	1977-78	969	561	11

Exhibit 1.2 : Distribution of Agricultural Requisites, Marketing of Agricultural Produce and Distribution of Consumer Goods by Cooperatives.

Year	Distribution of Agricultural Inputs (Rs. in crores)	Marketing of Agricultural produce (Rs. in crores)	Distribution of Consumer Goods (Rs. in crores)
1960-61	35.7	171	22.7
1965-66	121.1	360	198.1
1970-71	317.4	649	154.4
1971-72	364.8	844	180.1
1972-73	392.6	921	163.4
1973-74	479.7	1110	327.0
1974-75	711.3	1434	395.1
1975-76	818.1	1664	490.0
1976-77	851.2	1524	546.0
1977-78	1499.0	1834	624.0

Exhibit 1.3 : Statewise coverage of Membership, Milk Procurement and selected Infrastructure Facilities in Cooperative System, 1982-83.

State	No. of village coopera-tives	Farmer Milk Producer members	Milk pro-curement per day ('000 kgs.)	Artifi-cial Insemi-nation centres	Veteri-nary routes	Cattle feed Plant (Pub. & Coop.)*
NORTHERN REGION						
1. Haryana	988	96859	48.46	75	29	4
2. Rajasthan	1679	101168	275.02	177	30	5
3. Uttar Pradesh	588	53521	106.62	96	11	7
4. Punjab	2357	106726	384.57	286	38	1
SOUTHERN REGION						
5. Andhra Pradesh	1236	90900	635.25	19	11	6
6. Kerala	246	32958	25.05	-	8	-
7. Tamil Nadu	4024	666763	560.61	775	60	6
8. Karnataka	1803	266718	227.46	430	30	11
EASTERN REGION						
9. Assam	99	4400	1.34	-	1	-
10. Bihar	244	5896	24.47	-	-	1
11. Orissa	165	8674	6.69	64	6	-
12. West Bengal	723	28653	52.65	298	25	3
WESTERN REGION						
13. Gujarat	7033	989659	2075.91	660	132	7
14. Madhya Pradesh	1082	49003	393.73	280	30	7
15. Maharashtra	1072	112336	248.70	92	19	13
OTHER STATES & U.T.	170	13743	22.34	-	6	1
Total	23509	2627977	5092.87	3252	436	72

*Based on 1974 data.

Source: Annual Report 1982-83, National Dairy Development Board, Anand.

Exhibit 1.4 : Statewise Relative Share of Different Types of Milk Cooperatives, Their Membership and Milk Purchased, 1977-78.

	State	Type of Societies			Membership		Purchases				% of villages in the area of operation	
		State	Union	Soci-eties	Union	Soci-ety	Union		Society		Union	Society
							M	NM	M	NM		
1.	Andhra Pradesh	-	13.2	8.7	6.2	4.5	0.1	0.7	1.1	2.8	0.5	2.4
2.	Assam	-	0.6	0.1	-	0.1	-	-	0.1	0.1	-	0.1
3.	Bihar	-	-	1.5	-	0.4	-	-	0.1	0.1	-	0.6
4.	Gujarat	50.0	10.0	21.9	9.2	37.0	57.3	51.7	49.1	36.5	26.9	19.3
5.	Haryana	50.0	4.9	5.7	0.1	4.9	-	-	1.1	1.9	3.7	3.2
6.	Himachal Pradesh	-	0.5	0.2	0.1	0.1	-	0.1	0.1	0.3	-	0.8
7.	Jammu & Kashmir	-	-	0.1	-	0.1	-	-	0.1	-	-	0.2
8.	Karnataka	-	5.9	8.3	2.2	9.3	0.2	0.1	4.1	15.9	0.2	11.8
9.	Kerala	-	5.3	3.7	17.4	8.3	1.2	2.2	4.4	1.3	-	-
10.	Madhya Pradesh	-	-	3.5	-	1.0	-	-	1.1	1.8	-	2.7
11.	Maharashtra	-	42.6	23.8	29.1	24.2	31.2	16.2	30.4	24.9	49.7	27.2
12.	Orissa	-	3.0	0.9	0.1	0.5	0.5	-	0.2	0.3	0.7	4.7
13.	Punjab	-	3.6	10.0	0.1	3.7	1.3	19.5	1.1	8.0	3.7	4.6
14.	Rajasthan	-	5.3	7.8	0.1	3.7	7.2	6.2	4.9	4.0	9.9	7.9
15.	Tamil Nadu	-	-	-	-	-	-	-	-	-	-	-
16.	Uttar Pradesh	-	-	-	-	-	-	-	-	-	-	-
17.	West Bengal	-	2.6	2.7	9.1	1.1	0.5	-	1.3	1.3	3.5	2.6
18.	Other U.T.	-	2.5	1.1	26.3	1.1	0.5	4.2	0.8	0.8	1.2	11.9
Total/All India		100	100	100	100	100	100	100	100	100	100	100

M = Members NM = Non-Members

Source: Statistical statements relating to the cooperative movement in India Part II, Non-Credit Societies, Reserve Bank of India, Bombay, 1977-78.

Exhibit 1.5 : Cooperative Infrastructure of Milk Cooperatives in Gujarat and Maharashtra, 1982-83.

State	Districts	No. of village cooperatives	Members per society	Milk Procurement per day ('000 kg.)	Technical Assistance	
					A.I. centres	Veterinary Routes
GUJARAT	Banaskantha	1076	70	99	50	16
	Kaira	887	369	547	724	49
	Mehsana	887	180	455	835	31
	Sabarkantha	915	119	199	141	17
	Baroda	754	97	102	170	10
	Surat	627	137	128	38	9
	Bharuch	264	72	20	5	-
	Panchmahal	345	117	21	-	-
	Ahmedabad	256	55	47	-	1
	Rajkot	108	50	17	-	-
	Kutuh	43	12	4	-	1
	Bhavnagar	20	260	21	-	-
	Junagadh	132	34	8	19	-
	Valsad	187	-	7	-	-
MAHARASHTRA	Jalgaon	536	74	125	81	12
	Kolhapur	416	171	82	16	6

Only two district unions were functioning in Maharashtra.

Source: Annual Report of National Dairy Development Board, 1982-83.

Exhibit 1.6 : Distribution of Sample Dairy Farmers in Gujarat and Maharashtra.

Categorization Farmers	Jurisdiction of Dairy in Gujarat				Jurisdiction of Dairy in Maharashtra			
	Meh-sana Dist.	Sabar-kantha Dist.	Surat Dist.	Total	Warana-nagar (Kolhapur Dist.	Yal-guda	Miraj (Sangli Dist.)	Total
1. **Small** (Supplying milk less than 5 litres per day)								
(i) Members	32	25	38	95	39	75	19	133
(ii) Non-Members	8	12	-	20	12	11	10	33
2. **Medium** (Supplying milk between 5-10 litres per day)								
(i) Members	31	26	29	86	23	11	25	59
(ii) Non-Members	3	6	-	9	4	1	5	10
3. **Big** (Supplying milk more than 10 litres per day								
(i) Members	24	25	19	68	22	2	41	65
(ii) Non-Members	1	1	-	2	-	-	-	-
TOTAL				280				300
(i) Members	87	76	86	249	84	88	85	257
(ii) Non-Members	12	19	-	31	16	12	15	43

1. These also include industrial societies not dealing in agricultural produce, consumer stores nd housing societies.

2. Mathur and V.K. Gupta, Management in Cooperative Rice Mills, IIM, Ahmedabad, 1982.

3. The Dantwale Committee had recommended business of Rs. 5 lakh per year for economic viability of a cooperative marketing society. This amount was raised to Rs. 20 lakh in 1970.

4. Figures in brackets indicate the year of establishment.

TWO

RESOURCE STRUCTURE AND ITS UTILIZATION BY DAIRY FARMERS

2.1 Introduction

In view of the focus of the study to assess the economic and social gains that accrued due to vertical integration in milk commodity through a farmers' cooperative, an attempt is made in this chapter to find out, first, the resource position and its utilization by the sample dairy farmers. The interregion and intraregional variations in the prevailing situation will be examined separately for both members and non-members. This chapter analyses important structural characteristics, resource position and other socio-economic aspects in respect of the selected farmers, and the utilization of resources.

2.2 Livestock Resources

2.2.1 Composition of Herd

It would be desirable to have, first, a comprehensive view of livestock resources of the sample dairy farmers. The composition of livestock resources is given in Table 2.1.

The average size of herd comprising both bovine and ovine animals for members of a cooperative was 5.60 per household for sample dairy farmers in Gujarat and 5.10 per household in Maharashtra. Thus the member dairy farmers in Gujarat were having a slight advantage in ownership of total livestock resources as compared with sample farmers in Maharashtra. However, a comparison of members with non-members indicated that the average size of a herd of members of cooperative societies was larger than non-members in both States. Relatively sample dairy farmers (both

TABLE 2.1 : Distribution of Bovine and Ovine Animals among Different Categories of Sample Milk Suppliers in Gujarat and Maharashtra.

Particulars	Category of Milk Suppliers							
	Small		Medium		Big		Overall	
	M	NM	N	M	M	NM	M	NM
GUJARAT								
% of Bovine Animals to total	95.8	100.0	97.7	100.0	100.0	100.0	98.0	100.0
Bovine Animals Per Household	0.2	4.3	5.4	4.2	8.0	6.0	5.5	4.4
% of Ovine Animals to total	4.2	-	2.3	-	-	-	2.0	-
Ovine Animals per Household	0.2	-	0.1	-	-	-	0.1	-
Total (Bovine + Ovine)	100.0	100.0	100.0	100.0	100.0	100.0	100.0	100.0
Total Animals Per Household	4.0	4.3	5.5	4.2	8.0	6.0	5.6	4.4
MAHARASHTRA								
% of Bovine Animals to total	75.5	89.6	98.0	97.7	98.9	-	88.3	91.4
Bovine Animals Per Household	3.3	2.6	4.2	4.2	7.2	-	4.5	3.0
% of Ovine Animals to total	24.5	10.4	2.0	2.3	1.1	-	11.7	8.6
Ovine Animals Per Household	1.1	0.3	0.1	0.1	0.1	-	0.6	0.2
Total (Bovine + Ovine)	100.0	100.0	100.0	100.0	100.0	100.0	100.0	100.0
Total Animals Per Household	4.4	2.9	4.3	4.3	7.3	-	5.1	3.2

M = Member NM = Non-Member

members and non-members) in Gujarat had a higher herd size than those in Maharashtra.

Among different categories of member dairy farmers, per-household average herd size showed significant variations in the sample between small, medium and big farms of Gujarat. Small farms had 4 animals while medium and big farms had 5.5 and 8 respectively. However, in Maharashtra while there was little variation between the members in small and medium categories, herd size being 4.4 and 4.3 respectively, the big farms had on an average 7.3 animals. In respect of non-members, small and medium category farms had a similar size of herd (4.3 and 4.2 respectively) but the big category had an average of 6 animals per household in Gujarat. In Maharashtra small category households possessed 2.9 animals and medium category households 4.3 animals.

In terms of composition of the herd in two classes of animals, bovine and ovine, differences were observed between the sample dairy farmers of Gujarat and Maharashtra. Among the member dairy farmers, bovine animals constituted 98 per cent of the total in Gujarat as compared with 88.3 per cent in Maharashtra. Such differences were also observed among non-members and in Gujarat 100 per cent of the herd consisted of bovine animals while in Maharashtra it was 91.4 per cent.

As is evident from the above, among Gujarat farmers bovine animals dominated in all categories of farms. However, in the case of Maharashtra ovine animals to the extent 24.5 per cent existed in small category households amongst the members and 10.4 per cent in non-members. Medium and big category households had only 2.0 and 1.1 per cent ovine animals respectively.

2.2.2 Distribution of Milch Animals between Buffaloes and Cows:

Bovine animals could be classified between buffaloes and cows. It would be pertinent to find out the composition among sample dairy farmers. Further the composition of such animals changed in different seasons of the year, viz. monsoon, winter and summer. Taking these two situations, it was revealing that among members, the proportion of buffaloes in the herd size was around 95 per cent in

TABLE 2.2 : Distribution of Seasonwise Milch Animals (Buffaloes and Cows) among different Categories of Sample Milk Suppliers in Gujarat and Maharashtra.

(fig in %)

State	Category of Milk Supplier	Type of Milk Supplier	Distribution of Milch Animals in Different Seasons								
			Monsoon			Winter			Summer		
			Buffaloes	Cows	Total	Buffaloes	Cows	Total	Buffaloes	Cows	Total
GUJARAT											
	Small	M	94.5	5.5	100.0	93.9	6.1	100.0	95.5	4.5	100.0
		NM	82.2	17.8	100.0	82.6	17.4	100.0	87.5	12.5	100.0
	Medium	M	94.2	5.8	100.0	93.8	6.2	100.0	93.5	6.5	100.0
		NM	91.3	8.7	100.0	95.6	4.4	100.0	91.7	8.3	100.0
	Big	M	95.5	4.5	100.0	95.1	4.9	100.0	95.3	4.7	100.0
		NM	100.0	-	100.0	100.0	-	100.0	100.0	-	100.0
	Overall	M	94.8	5.2	100.0	94.3	5.7	100.0	94.7	5.3	100.0
		NM	86.1	13.9	100.0	87.8	12.2	100.0	89.7	11.3	100.0
MAHARASHTRA											
	Small	M	78.4	21.6	100.0	82.8	17.2	100.0	78.2	21.8	100.0
		NM	92.8	7.2	100.0	87.5	12.5	100.0	83.3	16.7	100.0
	Medium	M	46.9	53.1	100.0	46.1	53.9	100.0	39.8	60.2	100.0
		NM	73.3	26.7	100.0	73.3	26.7	100.0	80.0	20.0	100.0
	Big	M	38.3	61.7	100.0	34.7	65.3	100.0	29.7	70.3	100.0
		NM	-	-	-	-	-	-	-	-	-
	Overall	M	51.3	48.7	100.0	55.8	44.2	100.0	49.9	50.1	100.0
		NM	82.8	17.2	100.0	83.0	17.0	100.0	82.3	17.7	100.0

M = Member NM = Non-Member

Gujarat and between 50 and 56 per cent in Maharashtra (Table 2.2). However, no significant variation was observed in the proportion of buffaloes among non-members of both States. The proportion of buffaloes varied between 88 and 90 per cent in Gujarat and 82 and 83 per cent in Maharashtra amongst the non-members.

Among different categories of sample dairy farmers, regional and intraregional differences were marked. In Gujarat, among members and non-members, buffaloes constituted between 94 and 96 per cent of the total milch animals in small, medium and big categories of dairy farmers. However< in Maharashtra, the highest proportion of buffaloes were among small dairy member farmers and non-members and ranged between 78 and 83 per cent of the milch animals in three seasons. Big dairy members farmers of the cooperative had the highest proportion of cows which constituted 62 to 70 per cent of the milch animals in three seasons.

2.2.3 **Size of herd of milch animals**:

The next in order of importance is the assessment of herd size of the milch animals owned by the sample dairy farmers. This has been examined irrespective of ownership of type of milch animals, cow and buffalo.

The distribution of dairy farmers in the sample, according to the ownership of size of milch animal herd, indicated that the highest proportion of cooperative members owned two milch animals in Gujarat (31.7 per cent) and one milch animal in Maharashtra (40 per cent). However, among non-member dairy farmers, the highest proportion of these owned one milch animals in Gujarat (35.4 per cent) and Maharashtra (76.7 per cent). It appears that dairy farmers in Gujarat covered by the cooperative structure have shown preference for a large herd size. It is important to note that in Gujarat about 10 per cent of the sample farmers among members and non-members owned more than 5 milch animals as compared to 2.4 per cent of the sample farmers (only in member category) in Maharashtra (Table 2.3).

Certain similarities were also observed in the size ownership of milch animals in the selected regions of the study. For example, the

TABLE 2.3 : Distribution of Sample Milk Suppliers According to Ownership of Different Sizes of Milch Animals in Gujarat and Maharashtra.

(fig. in %)

State	Size of milch animals	Category of Milk Suppliers: Small M	Small NM	Medium M	Medium NM	Big M	Big NM	Total M	Total NM
GUJARAT									
	1	53.6	45.0	18.6	22.2	1.5	-	27.3	35.4
	2	36.8	15.0	39.5	33.3	14.7	50.0	31.7	22.5
	3	7.4	15.0	19.8	33.3	29.4	50.0	17.7	22.6
	4	1.1	15.0	16.3	-	26.5	-	13.3	9.7
	More than 5	1.1	10.0	5.8	11.2	27.9	-	10.0	9.7
MAHARASHTRA									
	1	58.6	87.9	27.1	40.0	12.3	-	39.7	76.7
	2	36.1	9.1	55.9	50.0	24.6	-	37.7	18.6
	3	5.3	3.0	11.9	10.0	32.3	-	13.6	4.7
	4	-	-	5.1	-	21.5	-	6.6	-
	More than 5	-	-	-	-	9.3	-	2.4	-
	Total	100.0	100.0	100.0	100.0	100.0	-	100.0	100.0

M = Member NM = Non Member

highest proportion of small farmers both members and non-members owned one milch animal. In the medium category of dairy farmers, the highest proportion of these owned two milch animals in both the categories. The highest proportion of big dairy farmers owned three milch animals in member category.

Another significant aspect to point out is that among members about 78 per cent in the sample owned three or less milch animals in Gujarat as compared with 91 per cent in Maharashtra. Among non-member small dairy farmers, about 88 per cent owned one milch animal in Maharashtra as compared to 45 per cent in Gujarat. Among small non-member dairy farmers, a tendency was observed in Gujarat to own a larger herd of milch animals. This was reflected by the fact that 40 per cent of such farmers owned more than three milch animals.

Thus the average size of herd varied considerably between the different categories of milk producers as well as between the States. As can be noted from Table 2.4, the average size of herd was 3.13, 4.40 and 6.80 between the small, medium and big size of **member** milk supplier categories in Gujarat. It is important to note that the herd size was smaller in the medium and big non-member category as compared to members. It was 3.44 and 4.50 respectively. However, in the small category the herd size was slightly greater (3.80) with the non-members in Gujarat. On the whole, Gujarat milch herd owners had larger number of animals than in Maharashtra. In Maharashtra, the number of milch animals per household were 2.72, 3.59 and 6.45 in small, medium and big category respectively amongst the members. Similarly, amongst the non-members it was 2.26, 3.60 amongst the small and medium category respectively.

An important aspect to note is the ratio between total milch animals and animals in milk per household. From Table 2.4, it can be further noted in this respect that the above ratio is also in favour of Gujarat as compared to Maharashtra both in respect of all categories of farmer members and non-members. An interesting aspect is the fact that the ratio was better for non-members as compared to members in both States and in all categories of milk suppliers. Further, the fact that in Maharashtra both amongst members

TABLE 2.4 : Size of Milch Animals and Animals in Milk among Different Categories of Sample Milk Suppliers in Gujarat and Maharashtra.

State	Category of milk supplier	Type	Per Household Size of Milch Animals: Buffaloes	Milch Animals: Cows	Milch Animals: Total	Animals in Milk: Buffaloes	Animals in Milk: Cows	Animals in Milk: Total	% of total animals in milk to total milch animals
GUJARAT									
	Small	M	2.91	0.22	3.13	1.45	0.11	1.56	50.2
		NM	3.20	0.60	3.80	2.00	0.40	2.40	63.2
	Medium	M	4.08	0.32	4.40	2.30	0.20	2.50	56.8
		NM	3.22	0.22	3.44	2.44	0.22	2.66	77.4
	Big	M	6.30	0.52	6.82	3.44	0.26	3.70	55.2
		NM	4.50	-	4.50	2.00	-	2.00	44.4
	Overall	M	4.24	0.34	4.58	2.28	0.18	2.46	54.0
		NM	3.29	0.45	3.74	2.12	0.32	2.44	65.5
MAHARASHTRA									
	Small	M	2.01	0.71	2.72	1.05	0.29	1.34	49.3
		NM	1.87	0.39	2.26	1.00	0.18	1.18	52.0
	Medium	M	1.44	2.15	3.59	0.79	1.13	1.92	53.8
		NM	2.70	0.90	3.60	1.20	0.40	1.60	44.4
	Big	M	1.81	4.64	6.45	0.98	2.23	3.21	49.8
		NM	-	-	-	-	-	-	-
	Overall	M	1.83	2.03	3.86	0.97	0.97	1.94	50.5
		NM	2.06	0.51	2.57	1.04	0.51	1.55	49.5

M = Member NM = Non-Member

and non-members in the medium and big category of milk suppliers, cows formed nearly half of the milch herd did not affect the above ratio.

TABLE 2.5 : Land Resources of Different Categories of Sample Milk Suppliers in Gujarat.

Category of Milk Suppliers	Type		Particulars	Distribution of Sample Farms and their 'Operational Land Size (Acres) No land	Below 5 Acres	5-10 Acres	10 Acres & above	Total/ Overall
Small	M	1.	Distribution	24.2	38.9	25.3	11.6	100.0
		2.	Av. Land Size	-	3.2	7.4	12.9	4.6
	NM	1.	Distribution	-	100.0	-		100.0
		2.	Av. Land Size	-	3.3	-	-	3.3
Medium	M	1.	Distribution	16.3	39.5	23.3	20.9	100.0
		2.	Av. Land Size	-	3.5	7.8	15.5	6.5
	NM	1.	Distribution	22.2	11.1	66.7	-	100.0
		2.	Av. Land Size	-	5.0	7.3	-	5.4
Big	M	1.	Distribution	8.8	36.8	20.6	33.8	100.0
		2.	Av. Land Size	-	3.1	8.0	14.0	7.7
	NM	1.	Distribution	-	-	-	100.0	100.0
		2.	Av. Land Size	-	-	-	16.0	16.0
Overall	M	1.	Distribution	17.3	38.5	23.3	20.9	100.0
		2.	Av. Land Size	-	3.3	7.7	14.5	6.1
	NM	1.	Distribution	22.5	51.6	19.4	6.5	100.0
		2.	Av. Land Size	-	3.4	7.3	16.0	4.3

M = Member NM = Non-Member

2.3 Land Resource

It may be emphasized that the size group of dairy producers is based upon the amount of milk supplied. It will be worth while to examine the relationship of operational holdings with the size class of milk producers. Among the members of the cooperatives, it was observed that about 17 per cent of the sample dairy farmers had no land in Gujarat as compared to about 10 per cent in Maharashtra. The distribution of non-members suggested that about 35 percent did not own land in Maharashtra as compared to 23 percent in

Gujarat. Thus, contrary to general belief, members of the cooperatives also included the landless in both States (Tables 2.5 and 2.6).

The distribution of the remaining cooperative member dairy farmers indicated that a majority of them owned land area up to five acres in Gujarat (39 per cent) and Maharashtra (61 per cent). The higher proportion of sample dairy farmers owning a small operational land area indicated the choice for cooperative approach for dairy development activities and to augment their income. But regional differences showed that sample dairy farmers were better endowed with land in Gujarat than in Maharashtra. The average operational landholding was 6.1 acres in Gujarat and 5.4 acres in

TABLE 2.6 : Land Resources of Different Categories of Sample Milk Suppliers in Maharashtra.

Category of Milk Suppliers	Type		Particulars	Distribution of Sample Farms and their Operational Land Size (Acres)				
				No land	Below 5 Acres	5-10 Acres	10 Acres & above	Total/ Overall
Small	M	1.	Distribution	10.5	67.7	18.0	3.8	100.0
		2.	Av. Land Size	-	2.6	7.2	14.8	4.4
	NM	1.	Distribution	42.4	45.5	9.1	3.0	100.0
		2.	Av. Land Size	-	1.6	6.6	16.0	1.5
Medium	M	1.	Distribution	6.8	64.4	22.0	6.8	100.0
		2.	Av. Land Size	-	3.0	8.0	12.2	4.5
	NM	1.	Distribution	10.0	70.0	10.0	10.0	100.0
		2.	Av. Land Size	-	2.5	8.0	15.0	4.1
Big	M	1.	Distribution	10.7	43.1	26.2	20.0	100.0
		2.	Av. Land Size	-	2.9	7.9	21.4	7.6
	NM	1.	Distribution	-	-	-	-	-
		2.	Av. Land Size	-	-	-	-	-
Overall	M	1.	Distribution	9.7	60.7	21.0	8.6	100.0
		2.	Av. Land Size	-	2.8	7.6	18.3	5.4
	NM	1.	Distribution	34.9	51.2	9.3	4.6	100.0
		2.	Av. Land Size	-	1.9	7.0	15.5	2.4

M = Member NM = Non-Member

Maharashtra. Among the different categories of dairy farmers, operational landholding tended to increase with increase in size of dairy farmers. This was applicable in both States. The implications are that big dairy suppliers also had large land resources. It needs to be noted, however, that even landless as well as small landholders also belonged to the big supplier category. In respect of non-members, the proportion of dairy farmers with no land resource was higher in Maharashtra (35 per cent) than in Gujarat (23 per cent). About 51 per cent of non-member dairy farmers in both States owned small landholdings (below five acres). As compared with members of cooperatives, non-members had a substantially lower average operational landholding in the sample. For the sample dairy farmers of Maharashtra, the average operational landholding size was 2.4 acres and 4.3 acres for Gujarat. However, the average operational land area for non-member dairy farmers also showed an increase with the increase in the size of dairy farms. However, the proportional increase in the land size is not of the same magnitude as the proportional increase in milk supplied; the former is less than latter.

2.4 Human Labour Resources

2.4.1 Size of Family

The source of labour supply for livestock and agriculture enterprise could be both from family and hired labour. An examination of family resources indicated that the average size of the family for member dairy farmers was higher in Gujarat (7.3 members) than in Maharashtra (6.8 members). However, non-members had a larger family in Maharashtra (6.4 members) than in Gujarat (5.9 members). Among different categories of sample dairy farmers, the average size of family was large among by dairy farmers. This was applicable for members as well as non-members of cooperatives (Table 2.6A).

TABLE 2.6A : Size of the Family among Different Categories of Sample Milk Suppliers in Gujarat and Maharashtra.

Category of Milk Suppliers	Gujarat M	Gujarat NM	Maharashtra M	Maharashtra NM
Small	7.2	5.1	6.6	6.2
Medium	6.8	6.2	6.3	6.8
Big	7.9	13.0	7.9	
Overall	7.3	5.0	6.8	6.4

M = Member NM = Non-Member

2.4.2 Other Social Characteristics of the Family

(a) **Composition of the Family:** Apart from the average size of the family, it is also important to know the distribution of sample farmers' families according to the norms of small and big families. The distribution of sample member farmers suggested the highest proportion of them had 4-6 members in Gujarat (43.0) as well as Maharashtra (47.9). A similar situation also existed among the sample families of non-members in both States. It appears the joint family system is still followed in the rural areas as about 19 per cent of the member farmer families in Maharashtra and about 17 per cent in Gujarat had more than 10 members in the family. However, the proportion of families having more than 10 members among non-member dairy farmers was relatively less in both States and in Gujarat it was only 6.5 per cent. The details of some of the important social characteristics are provided in Tables 2.7 and 2.8.

(b) **Caste Composition:** The caste composition of sample dairy farmers indicated predominance of one caste both in Gujarat and Maharashtra. In Gujarat, both among members and non-members, sample dairy farmers belonging to the Patel community constituted 68 and 77 per cent respectively. Similarly in Maharashtra, Marathas were predominant and constituted 60 per cent of the total member of families and 56 per cent of the total non-member families. The distribution of other caste groups indicated that the scheduled castes were quite important in the sample dairy farmers. In Gujarat these castes constituted 15 per cent of the total member farmers and 13 per cent of non-member farmers. However, in Maharashtra, the proportion of the scheduled castes was less than in Gujarat as they constituted 9 per cent among the member category and 12 per cent in the non-member category. However, with the initiation of programmes for the welfare of weaker sections, it is possible to reduce the impact of one particular community and to cover more families of the scheduled castes and tribes under the cooperative fold for daily development activities.

The representation of the scheduled caste/scheduled tribe people in the dairy cooperatives is, of course, dependent on the number of milch animals owned and any discrimination that may exist against this category. Both of these factors are usually against the

TABLE 2.7 : Social Characteristics of Different Categories of Sample Milk Suppliers in Gujarat.

(fig in %)

	Characteristics	Category of Milk Supplier Small		Medium		Big		Overall	
		M	NM	M	NM	M	NM	M	NM
1.	Composition of Family (100%)	100.0	100.0	100.0	100.0	100.0	100.0	100.0	100.0
	(a) Below 3 members	5.3	5.0	4.6	-	2.9	-	4.4	3.2
	(b) 4-6 members	38.9	80.0	52.3	78.0	36.8	-	43.0	74.2
	(c) 7-9 members	38.9	15.0	30.2	11.0	39.7	50.0	36.1	16.1
	(d) More than 10 members	16.9	-	12.9	11.0	20.6	50.0	16.5	6.5
2.	Distribution of Caste Groups (100%)	100.0	100.0	100.0	100.0	100.0	100.0	100.0	100.0
	(a) Patels	58.9	75.0	73.3	77.8	73.5	-	67.9	77.4
	(b) Intermediate Castes	15.8	10.0	14.0	-	20.6	-	16.5	6.5
	(c) Scheduled Castes	25.3	15.0	11.6	11.1	5.9	-	15.3	12.9
	(d) Others	-	-	1.1	11.1	-	-	0.3	3.2
3.	Respondent/Decision Makers								
	(a) Average Age	42.8	40.5	45.3	39.7	46.9	39.0	45.0	39.7
	(b) Educational Status (100%)	100.0	100.0	100.0	100.0	100.0	100.0	100.0	100.0
	(i) Illiterate	30.6	15.0	16.2	-	26.5	-	24.5	9.7
	(ii) Below Primary	14.7	10.0	14.0	-	5.9	-	12.1	6.5
	(iii) Below High School	14.7	-	12.8	-	8.8	-	12.4	-
	(iv) Primary	14.7	5.0	26.7	44.4	23.5	50.0	21.3	19.4
	(v) High School	14.7	40.0	20.1	33.3	16.2	-	17.7	35.4
	(vi) Above High School	10.6	30.0	8.2	22.3	19.1	50.0	12.0	29.0

M = Member NM = Non-Member

TABLE 2.8 : Social Characteristics of Different Categories of Sample Milk Suppliers in Maharashtra.

(fig. in %)

	Characteristics	Small M	Small NM	Medium M	Medium NM	Big M	Big NM	Overall M	Overall NM
1.	Composition of Family (100%)	100.0	100.0	100.0	100.0	100.0	-	100.0	100.0
	(a) Below 3 members	9.8	21.2	6.8	10.0	7.7	-	8.6	18.6
	(b) 4-6 members	53.4	33.3	55.9	20.0	29.2	-	47.9	30.2
	(c) 7-9 members	23.3	30.3	25.4	70.0	27.7	-	24.9	39.5
	(d) More than 10 members	13.5	15.2	11.9	-	35.4	-	18.6	11.7
2.	Distribution of Caste Groups (100%)	100.0	100.0	100.0	100.0	100.0	-	100.0	100.0
	(a) Marathas	57.1	54.5	54.2	60.0	63.1	-	60.0	55.8
	(b) Intermediate Castes	6.8	3.1	13.6	20.0	3.1	-	5.4	6.9
	(c) Scheduled Castes	12.8	12.1	5.1	10.0	4.6	-	8.9	11.7
	(d) Others	23.3	30.3	27.1	10.0	29.2	-	25.7	25.6
3.	Respondents/Decision-Makers								
	(a) Average Age	41.3	39.0	43.3	49.3	39.5	-	41.3	44.1
	(b) Educational Status (100%)	100.0	100.0	100.0	100.0	100.0	-	100.0	100.0
	(i) Illiterate	23.3	27.3	16.9	30.0	9.2	-	18.3	27.9
	(ii) Below Primary	16.5	21.2	11.9	10.0	6.2	-	12.8	18.6
	(iii) Primary	36.8	36.4	40.7	40.0	35.4	-	37.4	37.2
	(iv) Below High School	8.3	6.4	6.8	-	7.7	-	7.8	4.6
	(v) High School	10.5	9.0	15.2	-	33.8	-	17.5	7.0
	(vi) Above High School	4.6	-	8.5	20.0	7.7	-	6.2	4.7

M = Member NM = Non-Member

scheduled caste/scheduled tribe people. In spite of this, the fact that at least nine per cent of the members, in these States, come from the scheduled caste/scheduled tribe category shows that this otherwise historically ignored section of society is now getting an opportunity to gain from the efforts directed towards organizing rural producers. Furthermore, the percentage belonging to the scheduled caste/scheduled tribe non-member category is not higher than the member category. Thus, in these cooperatives as far as membership goes, there is no discrimination against the scheduled castes/scheduled tribes.

(c) **Educational Background:** Normally the head of the household or an elderly economically active person in the family decides the primary and/or subsidiary occupation to be followed by the family. It was considered desirable to ascertain the educational background of such a person in the family because they constituted the decision-makers in their dairy enterprise. The distribution of these decision-makers in the sample dairy farms indicated that they were middle-aged. The average age of a decision-maker of the family in Gujarat, however, was higher (45 years) than in Maharashtra (41.3 years). But among the non-members, the age of a decision-maker in the family was lower in Gujarat (39.7 years) than in Maharashtra (44.1 years).

With regard to the educational status of these decision-makers, it was observed that they were both illiterate and literate. In Gujarat about 25 per cent of the decision-makers in the member category were illiterate as compared to about 18 per cent in Maharashtra. In respect of non-members, illiterates were in a much higher proportion in Maharashtra (27.9 per cent) than in Gujarat (9.7 per cent). If matriculation is considered as the bare minimum required educational level, decision-makers among members and non-members of Gujarat had an advantage over their counterparts in Maharashtra. In Gujarat about 30 per cent in the member category and about 64 per cent in the non-member category had attained education up to high school and beyond high school level. In contrast, in Maharashtra only about 24 per cent of the decision-makers in the member category and about 12 per cent in the non-member category had received education up to high school and above high school level. Among the different categories

TABLE 2.9 : Occupational Pattern (Primary and Subsidiary) of Different Categories of Sample Milk Suppliers in Gujarat.
(Fig in %)

Category of Dairy Farmers	Primary Occupation						Subsidiary Occupation				
	Agri-culture	Dairy	Ser-vice	Busi-ness	Lab-our	Total	Agri-culture	Dairy	Profe-ssionals	No occu-pation	Total
a. Small											
(i) M	56.8	30.5	9.5	-	3.2	100.0	26.3	47.4	14.7	11.6	100.0
(ii) NM	35.0	30.0	30.0	5.0	-	100.0	30.0	20.0	-	50.0	100.0
b.Medium											
(i) M	53.5	34.5	3.5	1.5	7.0	100.0	27.9	52.3	4.7	15.1	100.0
(ii) NM	33.4	44.4	11.1	11.5	-	100.0	66.7	11.1	-	22.2	100.0
c. Big											
(i) M	72.1	23.5	4.4	-	-	100.0	29.4	35.3	17.7	17.6	100.0
(ii) NM	50.0	-	50.0	-	-	100.0	50.0	50.0	-	-	100.0
d.Overall/Total											
(i) M	59.8	30.1	6.0	0.5	3.6	100.0	27.7	45.8	12.3	14.5	100.0
(ii) NM	35.5	32.2	25.8	6.5	-	100.0	41.9	19.3	-	38.8	100.0

M = Member NM = Non-Member

of member dairy farmers, relatively the proportion of decision-makers in the big category with education of high school and above high school was higher (35 per cent) than in the small category of dairy farmers (25 per cent) in Gujarat. Among the non-member category, the proportion of decision-makers in the big category was 50 per cent as compared to 70 per cent in the small category. A similar situation also prevailed in Maharashtra. However, it appears that a high proportion of decision-makers in the small category was a welcome feature and it would be possible to bring them round to agree to change of technology in the dairy field by showing them the advantages of the cooperative approach in dairy development activities.

(d) **Occupation:** Along with demographic characteristics and educational status of decision-makers, it is also important to find out the primary and secondary occupational structures of sample dairy farmers. Among the sample dairy farmers along with agriculture, business, service, dairying was the primary occupation of about 30 per cent members and 32 per cent non-members in Gujarat (Table 2.9). Further, among the various subsidiary occupations, 46 per cent members and 19 per cent non-members had indicated dairying as their subsidiary occupation. In Maharashtra, dairying was the primary occupation of only 5 per cent members and 2 per cent non-members (Table 2.10). Dairying as a subsidiary occupation was admitted by about 28 per cent members and about 35 per cent non-members. Thus agriculture was still the major occupation of the majority of sample dairy farmers in Maharashtra.

In both States, as the farm size increased, so did the percentage of farmers reporting agriculture as their primary occupation. Considering the secondary occupation, the same is the picture for dairying in Maharashtra, while in Gujarat the picture is mixed. Particularly in Maharashtra, the smaller the size of the dairy farm the larger the percentage of farmers reporting no secondary occupation.

Among different categories of dairy farmers, the medium category of dairy farmers had followed dairying as the primary occupation in a higher proportion than small and big dairy farmers in Gujarat. This was both in respect of members and non-members. A similar situation also existed in Maharashtra.

TABLE 2.10 : Occupational Pattern (Primary and Subsidiary) of Different Categories of Sample Milk Suppliers in Maharashtra.

(Fig in %)

Category of Dairy Farmers	Primary Occupation						Subsidiary Occupation				
	Agriculture	Dairy	Service	Business	Labour	Total	Agriculture	Dairy	Professionals	No occupation	Total
a. Small											
(i) M	82.7	3.0	9.0	5.3	-	100.0	6.8	12.8	5.3	75.1	100.0
(ii) NM	54.5	3.1	24.2	12.1	6.1	100.0	18.2	30.3	3.0	48.5	100.0
b.Medium											
(i) M	78.0	8.5	11.9	-	1.6	100.0	11.9	30.5	3.4	54.2	100.0
(ii) NM	70.0	-	30.0	-	-	100.0	-	50.0	-	50.0	100.0
c. Big											
(i) M	89.2	6.2	1.5	3.1	-	100.0	4.6	58.5	-	36.9	100.0
(ii) NM	-	-	-	-	-	-	-	-	-	-	-
d.Overall/Total											
(i) M	83.3	5.1	7.8	3.5	0.3	100.0	7.4	28.4	3.5	60.7	100.0
(ii) NM	58.1	2.3	25.6	9.3	4.7	100.0	13.9	34.9	2.4	48.8	100.0

M = Member NM = Non-Member

The above prevailing situation has implications with respect to the income generation at the farm level, from the mix of crop and dairy husbandry. In Maharashtra, there is sufficient scope to motivate people to follow dairying as an enterprise to augment their resources, and the cooperative conception could provide impetus to the development of dairying as a secondary activity. Second, non-member dairy farmers could easily be persuaded to strengthen and quicken the process of cooperativization in dairying because non-members might not have joined cooperatives due to lack of interest or owing to the failure of cooperative leadership to influence them. Third, in Gujarat, since a substantial number of small farmers (20.5 to 47.4 per cent) have dairying as either primary or secondary occupation, the possibility of increasing incomes of small farmers through the dairy cooperatives is very high. In contrast, since very few small farmers reported (9.0 to 12.8 per cent) dairying as either primary or secondary occupation, in Maharashtra, it is unlikely that integrated dairy cooperatives alone can increase their incomes substantially; unless the basic assets are provided for the milk production which would induce the farmers to make dairying either the primary or secondary occupation.

(a) **Membership of Cooperatives:** We had asked farmers some questions concerning their participation in cooperatives other than dairy. Table 2.11 shows that in this respect there is also a difference between the sample farmers in Gujarat and Maharashtra. In Gujarat, only 10 per cent of the dairy farmers are members of both dairy and other cooperatives, while in Maharashtra they are 63.4 per cent of the total sample size. In Gujarat, non-members do not belong to other cooperatives. In contrast, Maharashtra has 42 per cent of non-members who are members of other cooperatives. The major reason behind this is that the districts surveyed, namely, Sangli and Kolhapur, have sugarcane as their main cash crop, where sugar cooperatives are well established. Out of the sample districts in Gujarat, only in Surat district, where sugarcane has been extensively cultivated, do sugar cooperatives exist.

In both States a relatively large number of big producers are members of both types of cooperatives. In Maharashtra, 80 per cent of big producers are members of dairy as well as sugar cooperatives, while in Gujarat their percentage is only 10. Thus,

TABLE 2.11 : Participation of Different Categories of Sample Milk Suppliers in Cooperative Activities.

Particulars	Category of Dairy Farmers in Gujarat				Category of Dairy Farmers in Maharashtra			
	Small	Medium	Big	Total	Small	Medium	Big	Total
1. Total Sample								
a. M	95	86	68	249	133	59	65	257
b. NM	20	9	2	31	33	10	-	43
2. Membership of Dairy Farmers in Co-operative other than Dairy (% to total category)								
a. M	6.3	11.6	13.2	10.0	52.6	69.5	80.0	63.4
b. NM	-	-	-	-	36.4	60.0	-	41.9
3. Per-household value of share (Rs.) in the category of*								
a. M								
(i) in Dairy Coop.	157.50	190.50	290.70	**205.29**	45.70	156.10	331.10	**143.79**
(ii) in Other Coop.	1433.30	681.00	1333.30	**1096.40**	751.60	1158.00	1346.40	**1043.55**
b. NM								
(i) in Dairy Coop.	-	-	-	-	-	-	-	-
(ii) in Other Coop.	-	-	-	-	449.10	1053.50	-	650.56

* at the time of survey in August-September, 1982.

M = Member NM = Non-Member

Maharashtra presents a better picture of membership in dairy and other cooperatives compared to Gujarat. It should be noted, this is a result of the types of crops grown, and this difference between the two States cannot be attributed to the performance of cooperatives.

Gujarat presents a better picture in terms of the value of shares owned by farmers in dairy cooperatives (Table 2.11). Here the members owned, on an average, Rs.205 worth of shares, while in Maharashtra only Rs.143 worth of shares were held by the member producers. In both States, the value of shares held increased as the size class of dairy producers increased.

At the same time, the value of shares held in other cooperatives was much higher than the value of shares held in dairy cooperatives in both States. This is again due to sugar cooperatives in which some producers were members. The average value of shares held in sugar cooperatives was the same in both States. In Gujarat, there is no correlation between the size class and the value of shares owned for sugar cooperatives, while in Maharashtra, the value increased as the size class increased.

2.4.3 Capital Resources

Capital investments made by the sample dairy farmers were grouped into five broad categories: land, residential buildings, farm house, irrigation, power and other farm equipments, milch animals and other draught and young stock. Investment of the households in securities, precious metals and consumer durables was not included.

About two-thirds of the investment by member farmers in Gujarat was in land, farm house, irrigation, power and other farm equipments as compared with three-fourths in Maharashtra. Among the non-member category of sample dairy farmers, investment in the above items similarly did not exceed more than two-thirds of the total investments in Gujarat (68.2 per cent). This was higher than in Maharashtra (62.2 per cent). Thus, in terms of total assets, Gujarat presented a better picture than Maharashtra. Furthermore, the members of dairy cooperatives, in both States, owned more assets than non-members. The details are provided in Tables 2.12 and 2.13.

TABLE 2.12 : Per-Household Value of Owned Assets among Different Categories of Milk Suppliers in Gujarat.

(in Rs.)

Category		Irrigation, Power and	Milch Animals other equip-ments	Other Animals	Total Animals	Land	Resi-dential	Farm Houses Houses	Total
Small	M	21262	4988	4230	9218	38895	25935	2559	97869
		(21.72)*	(5.10)	(4.32)	(9.42)	(39.74)	(26.50)	(2.62)	(100.00)
	NM	21150	7175	3505	10680	20150	25565	700	78245
		(27.03)	(9.19)	(4.46)	(13.65)	(25.75)	(32.67)	(0.90)	(100.00)
Medium	M	39719	8577	4932	13509	48535	34872	1643	138278
		(28.72)	(6.20)	(3.57)	(9.77)	(35.10)	(25.22)	(1.19)	(100.00)
	NM	20311	9178	4378	13556	29778	41556	3333	108534
		(18.71)	(8.46)	(4.03)	(12.49)	(27.44)	(38.29)	(3.07)	(100.00)
Big	M	39638	13593	7100	20693	80676	53382	1590	196079
		(20.22)	(6.98)	(3.62)	(10.60)	(41.14)	(27.22)	(0.82)	(100.00)
	NM	70700	5250	16650	21900	110000	59000	5000	266600
		(26.52)	(1.97)	(6.24)	(8.21)	(41.26)	(22.13)	(1.88)	(100.00)
Total	M	32655	8609	5053	13862	53635	36517	1978	138647
		(23.55)	(6.21)	(3.79)	(10.00)	(38.68)	(26.34)	(1.43)	(100.00)
	NM	24103	7665	4574	12239	28742	32365	1742	99191
		(24.30)	(7.73)	(4.61)	(12.34)	(28.98)	(32.63)	(1.76)	(100.00)

* Figures in parentheses are the percentage share of the value of different assets in the total value of assets.

M = Member NM = Non-Member

TABLE 2.13 : Per-Household Value of Capital Assets among Different Categories of Milk Suppliers in Maharashtra.

(in Rs.)

Category of Dairy Farmer		Irrigation, Power and other equipments	Milch Animals	Other Animals	Total Animals	Land	Residential Houses	Farm Houses	Total
Small	M	10109 (15.4)	2897 (4.4)	3000 (4.6)	5897 (9.0)	36838 (56.3)	11915 (18.2)	710 (1.1)	65469 (100.0)
	NM	3500 (7.8)	2582 (5.8)	1722 (3.9)	4304 (9.7)	19454 (43.8)	16903 (38.1)	257 (0.6)	44418 (100.0)
Medium	M	14785 (13.6)	5539 (5.1)	3166 (2.9)	8705 (8.0)	63389 (58.5)	19474 (18.0)	2069 (1.9)	108426 (100.0)
	NM	12300 (13.9)	3910 (4.4)	2055 (2.3)	5965 (6.7)	57400 (64.8)	12700 (14.4)	200 (0.2)	88565 (100.0)
Big	M	31367 (15.3)	10017 (4.9)	5714 (2.8)	15731 (7.7)	124415 (60.8)	31506 (15.4)	1593 (0.8)	204612 (100.0)
	NM	-	-	-	-	-	-	-	-
Overall	M	16559 (15.0)	5296 (4.8)	3733 (3.4)	9029 (8.2)	65083 (58.9)	18605 (16.8)	1245 (1.1)	110521 (100.0)
	NM	5546 (10.1)	2891 (5.3)	1799 (3.3)	4690 (8.6)	28279 (51.7)	15925 (29.2)	245 (0.4)	54685 (100.0)

Note: Figures in parentheses are the percentage share of the value of different assets in the total value of assets.
M = Member NM = Non-Member

Investment in residential houses was the next item of importance. The proportion of such investment to the total varied between 23.1 and 24.6 per cent among the non-member and member category of dairy farmers in Gujarat. Contrary to a small variation in the investments in residential houses in Gujarat, wide variations were observed in the proportion of such investments among the member and non-member category in Maharashtra. The proportion of such investment was about 17 per cent in the member category of sample dairy farmers as compared with 29 per cent among non-members.

Despite the fact that dairying was the primary and subsidiary occupation of significant proportion of the selected households, investment in total livestock resources was less than 10 per cent in both States. The proportion of investment in livestock resource did not vary significantly in the two category of member and non-member sample dairy farmers. A similar situation was prevalent in respect of investments in milch animals also and it was varying around 5 per cent among the member and non-member category of sample dairy farmers in the two States.

It would be pertinent to examine the qualitative aspect of milch animals of the sample dairy farmers in terms of present market money value. The per-household value of a milch animals was higher in Gujarat (Rs.8,609) than in Maharashtra (Rs.5,269) for member dairy farmers. A similar situation prevailed among the non-members also but strikingly the per-household money value in Maharashtra (Rs.2,891) was significantly lower than in Gujarat (Rs.7,665). It appears that the qualitative aspect of the breed of milch animals has a say in the lower value of milch animals in Maharashtra than in Gujarat. It needs to be noted that Gujarat had a larger number of milch animals per member household (4.05) and non-member household (3.74) as compared to Maharashtra member and non-member households having 3.86 and 2.57 respectively. Further, Gujarat farmers in all categories had dominantly buffaloes as milch animals while the Maharashtra farmers, particularly in the medium and large category, had a high proportion of cows.

Among the different categories of sample farmers, per-household total investment was the lowest among small dairy farmers and the highest in big dairy farmers. This was applicable to both member and non-member categories of sample dairy farmers in both States. A similar situation was observed also in respect of value of milch animal per household in both States.

However, the pattern of investment of sample dairy farmers indicated no substantial variations in the type of investments, and diversifications were expected particularly from the cooperative member dairy farmers. Further, the proportion of investment in milch animals was quite small and with the development of dairy activities, it is expected that cooperative members in the small category at least would like to double this proportion to augment their income.

2.5 **Resource Utilization**

2.5.1 **Human Resource**

Since labour supply for an enterprise could be from both family and hired sources, an attempt is made to examine involvement of

TABLE 2.14 : Involvement of Family and Hired Labour among Different Categories of Milk Suppliers in Gujarat and Maharashtra.

Category		Family Labour (mandays) (per household)	Hired Labour (mandays)	Total (mandays)
GUJARAT				
Small	M	557	100	657
	NM	447	164	611
Medium	M	579	170	749
	NM	162	-	162
Big	M	654	419	1063
	NM	730	-	730
Overall	M	591	211	802
	NM	388	235	623
MAHARASHTRA				
Small	M	444	22	466
	NM	498	33	531
Medium	M	563	210	773
	NM	511	109	620
Big	M	685	354	1039
	NM	-	-	-
Overall	M	532	149	681
	NM	500	42	542

M = Member NM = Non-Member

TABLE 2.15 : Proportion of Adult and Child Family Labour in Milk Production among Different Categories of Sample Milk Suppliers in Gujarat and Maharashtra.

State	Family Labour					
	Adult Male	Adult Female	Child-ren	Total	Hired Labour	Total Labour
GUJARAT						
Small	178	113	266	554	100	657
	(27.09)	(17.20)	(40.48)	(84.77)	(15.23)	(100.00)
Medium	171	112	296	579	170	749
	(22.83)	(14.95)	(39.52)	(77.30)	(22.70)	(100.00)
Big	137	162	355	654	419	1073
	(12.77)	(15.10)	(33.08)	(60.95)	(39.05)	(100.00)
Overall	164	126	301	591	211	802
	(20.45)	(15.71)	(37.53)	(73.69)	(26.31)	(100.00)
MAHARASHTRA						
Small	155	45	244	444	22	466
	(33.26)	(9.66)	(52.36)	(95.28)	(4.72)	(100.00)
Medium	197	58	308	563	210	773
	(25.49)	(7.50)	(39.84)	(72.83)	(27.17)	(100.00)
Big	191	74	420	685	354	1039
	(18.38)	(7.12)	(40.42)	(65.92)	(34.08)	(100.00)
Overall	174	55	303	532	149	681
	(25.55)	(8.08)	(44.49)	(78.12)	(21.88)	(100.00)

Figures in parentheses are percentages to total.

family members in terms of time devoted for dairy enterprise and also the extent of hired labour among the sample dairy farmers. Also generally both adults and children of both sexes in the rural areas devote time to dairying activity, involving cleaning of cattleshed, grazing and feeding of livestock, milking and marketing of milk products. We have estimated the extent of time devoted by the family and hired labour resources separately.

2.5.1.1 **Utilization of Family Resources**

The total time devoted by the family members (male or female) was converted into mandays to measure the capacity of employment generation in dairy enterprises. Female labour was treated on a par otal time devoted by the family members (male or female) was converted into mandays to measure the capacity of employment generation in dairy enterprises. Female labour was treated on a par with male labour in this respect. In the two regions, the sample farmers devoted 591 mandays per family in gujarat and about 532 mandays in Maharashtra in the dairying activity. However among non-members per-family mandays devoted to dairying were more in

Maharashtra (500 mandays) than in Gujarat (388 mandays) (Table 2.14).

It is important to note that in Maharashtra, even though the percentage of adult females is higher (30.98) than in Gujarat (25.79), the contribution of the adult female labour input is low (Table 2.16). The opposite is the case for children in the two States.

2.5.1.2 **Utilization of Hired Labour**

Closely linked with the involvement of family resources was the hiring of labour to undertake various activities. In Gujarat, both family and hired labour was utilized in greater magnitude than in Maharashtra. In Gujarat, the estimated per-household mandays of hired labour per household were 211 and 235 for member and non-member dairy farmers respectively. In Maharashtra, they were 149 and 42 mandays per household for member and non-member dairy farmers respectively (Table 2.14).

It is important to note that the total mandays spent per household on dairy increased with increase in the quantum of milk supply amongst both member and non-member categories in both States.

The share of hired labour in total labour was higher in Gujarat than in Maharashtra. In both States as the size of dairy increased the share of hired labour also increased.

TABLE 2.16 : Percentage of Male and Female Population in Gujarat and Maharashtra.

State	Adults[1]		Children[2]		All		
	Male	Female	Male	Female	Male	Female	Total
Gujarat	32.60	25.79	23.48	18.13	56.08	43.92	100.00
Maharashtra	35.59	30.98	19.21	14.22	54.80	45.20	100.00

*This is for members and non-members together.

[1] Adults are of age greater than or equal to 18.
[2] Children are of age less than 18.

2.5.1.3 Labour Utilization Per Milch Animal

We attempted to examine labour utilization per milch animal to observe the extent of labour use and to understand if economies of scale operated in this regard. As can be noted from table 2.17 Gujarat used 169 mandays per milch animal as compared to Maharashtra's only 150 mandays among member category farmers. However, in the case of non-members, Maharashtra used more mandays (204) than Gujarat (165). It is interesting to note that in the total mandays used per milch animal about 24 per cent were hired mandays amongst the member category farmers in Gujarat and Maharashtra. Amongst the non-members hired labour constituted 34 per cent in Gujarat as against only 6 per cent in Maharashtra. Thus hired labour was a significant feature in Gujarat only.

The use of total mandays spent per milch animal varied with the quantity of milk supplied represented by the different categories of suppliers amongst both member and non-member categories in Gujarat. The contrast is quite significant as the small category used 209 mandays per milch animal annually as compared to only 158 days by the big category supplier amongst members in Gujarat. It must be remembered that the data from non-members in this regard were not very reliable as the number of observations was very small. The situation in this regard was not very clear in the case of Maharashtra. There, the small category supplier used 170 mandays per milch animal as compared to the big supplier using 161 mandays and the medium category using 215 mandays. It does seem that economies of scale do operate.

2.5.2 Land Resource

Some of thc most important characteristics features of the land utilization pattern of sample dairy farmers in Gujarat and Maharashtra are described below:

TABLE 2.17 : Involvement of Family and Hired Labour among Sample Respondents in Gujarat and Maharashtra (per milch animal).

Category of milk suppliers		Family Labour (mandays)	Hired Labour (mandays)	Total (mandays)
GUJARAT				
Small	M	177	32	209
	NM	118	43	161
Medium	M	131	39	170
	NM	47	-	47
Big	M	96	62	158
	NM	162	-	162
Overall	M	129	40	169
	NM	102	53	155
MAHARASHTRA				
Small	M	162	8	170
	NM	219	15	234
Medium	M	157	58	215
	NM	142	30	172
Big	M	106	55	161
	NM	-	-	-
Overall	M	138	45	183
	NM	194	13	207

M = Member NM = Non-Member

2.5.2.1 Cropping Pattern

Significant variations were observed in the cropping pattern of the sample dairy farmers in Gujarat and Maharashtra. In Gujarat, the cropping pattern of the sample dairy farmers was more oriented towards raising subsistence crops. The area under cereal crops accounted for 84 per cent of the gross cropped area for the member category and 90 per cent for the non-member category. In Maharashtra, the proportion of area under cereal crops was about 48 per cent for the member category and 39 per cent for the non-member category (Table 2.18).

Among the different categories of dairy farmers, no significant variations were observed in the proportion of area devoted to cereal crops in Maharashtra. However, small dairy farmers in Gujarat relatively devoted a larger proportion of area under cereal crops than the big dairy farmers in both categories. It may, however, be mentioned that more than 50 per cent of the gross cropped area in Maharashtra was under sugarcane which was the principal crop. We have already stated elsewhere that the selected milk cooperatives were in fact initiated by the sugar cooperative in Maharashtra.

TABLE 2.18 : Land Utilization Characteristics of Different Categories of Sample Milk Suppliers in Gujarat and Maharashtra.

State	Category of Milk suppliers	Type of farmers	Cropping* intensity (%)	Proportion of area under cereal crops to Gross cropped area (%)	Proportion of area under cash crops to Gross cropped area (%)
GUJARAT					
	Small	M	137.1	91.2	4.4
		NM	123.2	92.8	-
	Medium	M	155.1	82.6	8.2
		NM	174.2	96.3	-
	Big	M	158.9	83.1	13.3
		NM	229.2	81.8	18.2
	Overall	M	150.4	84.2	9.1
		NM	160.4	90.4	5.6
MAHARASHTRA					
	Small	M	123.1	47.3	52.7
		NM	101.3	37.7	62.3
	Medium	M	137.0	50.4	49.6
		NM	103.1	40.3	59.7
	Big	M	137.8	47.4	52.6
		NM	-	-	-
	Overall	M	131.4	47.5	52.5
		NM	102.7	38.5	61.5

* Cropping intensity is the proportion of Gross cropped area to Net area sown.

M = Member NM = Non-Member

2.5.2.2 Cropping Intensity

The ratio of gross cropped area to net cropped area was computed for difficult sizes of sample dairy farmers.

The cropping intensity of the sample dairy farmers among both categories was higher in Gujarat than in Maharashtra. As already referred earlier, the lower cropping intensity in Maharashtra was due to dairy farmers' preference for raising sugarcane.

2.5.2.3 Availability of Fodder from Farm Resources

Rearing of livestock required sufficient quantity of dry and green fodder for their maintenance. Experience had shown that farmers were generally more dependent for fodder supply from their own farm resources. An attempt is made in this section to examine the acreage of fodder-bearing crops per reared animal and to estimate the quantity of fodder available from the cropped acreage per day.

Apparently dairy farmers in Gujarat had higher acreage of fodder-bearing crops both per cattle and per milch animal than in Maharashtra (Table 2.19). This position was observed in the case of member and non-member dairy farmers. Since the requirements were for both green and dry fodder, it was difficult to apportion these and the estimates were attempted for dry fodder only. It was observed that per-day availability of dry fodder from the farm resources was about 16 kg and 13 kg per milch animal for member and non-member dairy farmers respectively in Gujarat. Availability per milch animal was merely 4 kg per day for both member and non-member dairy farmers in Maharashtra. If we compare the availability with the per-day average consumption requirement of dry fodder of about 12 kg per milch animal, dairy farmers in Maharashtra were at a great disadvantage.

2.5.2.4 **Milk Production**

Earlier in the chapter the ownership pattern of bovine and milch animals and their distribution between buffaloes and cows was discussed. In this section, an attempt is made to examine the milk production pattern of the sample dairy farmers. It would have been ideal to understand the milk production pattern and aspects of animal productivity keeping in view the breed aspects of milch animals, calving months, lactation period and intervals between two calvings. But due to the paucity of data and to keep uniformity in the two selected regions, seasonwise milk production pattern per household only has been attempted. Since composition of milch animals varied in the different seasons, seasonwise availability of milk has also been discussed in the following paragraphs.

Various environmental and management aspects significantly influence the productivity of milch animals and consequently the availability of milk to the household. Seasonwise per-household availability of milk and the total during the reference period of the study is provided in Table 2.20.

Per-household total availability of milk from milch animals during three seasons was much higher in Gujarat (3,178 litres) than in Maharashtra (2,719 litres) for the member category of households. A similar situation also prevailed for the non-member category of households and perhousehold availability from production was 2,118 litres in Gujarat and 1,238 litres in Maharashtra. Among the different categories of milk producers, among members, small milk producers in Gujarat had

Table 2.19 : Availability of Fodder from Farm Resources among Different Categories of Milk Suppliers in Gujarat and Maharashtra.

States	Category of Milk Suppliers	Type of farmers	Area under fodder bearing crops Per cattle (Acres)	Per Milch Animal (Acres)	Estimated Total* quantity of fodder per milch animal available from farm resource in crop seasons per day (kgs.)
GUJARAT					
	Small	M	1.56	3.10	14.8
		NM	0.88	1.40	9.8
	Medium	M	1.78	2.61	22.4
		NM	1.74	2.25	15.1
	Big	M	1.36	2.51	12.2
		NM	5.00	11.25	38.5
	Overall	M	1.55	2.87	16.3
		NM	1.43	2.18	13.4
MAHARASHTRA					
	Small	M	0.61	1.23	4.3
		NM	0.59	1.12	3.8
	Medium	M	0.80	1.49	5.5
		NM	0.51	1.16	3.4
	Big	M	0.74	1.50	3.4
		NM	-	-	-
	Overall	M	0.77	1.41	4.2
		NM	0.56	1.14	3.6

*If the total number of animals were taken into account the availability of fodder per animal would considerably decline.
M = Member NM = Non-Member

logically the lowest per-household availability from production and the big milk producers the highest. Precisely, in the member category, big milk producers were having three times more per-household availability from production than that of small milk producers. A near similar situation prevailed for non-members also in Gujarat and for members and non-members in Maharashtra.

Seasonwise per-household availability from production of milk for members and non-members of different categories of producers indicated the monsoon season as the peak period of milk availability in Gujarat. Though the peak period of milk availability on an average was highest in the monsoon season for both members and non-members, the pattern changed in different categories of milk producers. This was due to changes in the lactation period of different types of milch animals.

TABLE 2.20 : Per-Household Production of Milk among Different Categories of Sample Milk Suppliers in Gujarat and Maharashtra.

(in litres)

State	Category of Milk suppliers	Type of Milk suppliers	Seasons during the year Winter	Summer	Monsoon	Total during the year
GUJARAT						
	Small	M	625	525	395	1545
		NM	634	588	417	1639
	Medium	M	990	966	809	2765
		NM	994	894	891	2779
	Big	M	2294	1995	1691	5980
		NM	1320	1520	1100	3940
	Overall	M	1207	1079	892	**3178**
		NM	782	737	599	**2118**
MAHARASHTRA						
	Small	M	309	362	381	1052
		NM	164	328	429	**921**
	Medium	M	850	891	1095	2836
		NM	732	735	817	**2284**
	Big	M	2217	1820	1987	6024
		NM	-	-	-	-
	Overall	M	916	852	951	**2719**
		NM	296	423	519	**1238**

M = Member NM = Non-Member

Interestingly, as observed earlier in the ownership pattern of milch animals, buffaloes provided a higher proportion of milk in Gujarat for both member and non-member categories of dairy farmers. The extent of availability of milk from buffaloes was as high as 96 per cent for member and 87 per cent for non-member category of dairy farmers in Gujarat (Table 2.21). In Maharashtra, the major source was cows. Among the different sizes of dairy farmers, small farmers had the highest proportion of milk supplies from buffaloes (75 per cent) and big farmers only 16 per cent.

Table 2.21 : Proportion of Buffalo and Cow Milk Production among Different Categories of Milk Suppliers in Gujarat and Maharashtra.

State	Category of Milk Suppliers	Type of Milk Suppliers	Monsoon B	Monsoon C	Winter B	Winter C	Summer B	Summer C	Total B	Total C
GUJARAT										
	Small	M	96	4	94	6	96	4	95	5
		NM	81	19	79	21	82	18	80	20
	Medium	M	96	4	95	5	96	4	96	4
		NM	89	11	95	5	92	8	92	8
	Big	M	96	4	96	4	96	4	96	4
		NM	100	-	100	-	100	-	100	-
	Overall	M	96	4	95	5	96	4	96	4
		NM	86	14	88	12	88	12	87	13
MAHARASHTRA										
	Small	M	76	24	80	20	68	32	75	25
		NM	81	19	88	12	88	12	84	16
	Medium	M	38	62	40	60	22	78	33	67
		NM	69	31	68	32	67	33	68	32
	Big	M	12	88	20	80	16	84	16	84
		NM	-	-	-	-	-	-	-	-
	Overall	M	49	51	38	62	29	71	32	68
		NM	74	26	80	20	76	24	77	23

B = Buffaloes C = Cows
M = Member NM = Non-Member

Among non-members, however, buffaloes contributed more than cows among the sample dairy farmers.A similar situation also prevailed in different sizes of milk producers. Therefore, it may perhaps be said that medium and big dairy farmers in Maharashtra had preference for rearing cows whereas small-size dairy farmers relied primarily on buffaloes.

THREE

ECONOMICS OF MILK PRODUCTION AMONG SAMPLE MILK SUPPLIERS

3.1 Introduction

The discussion in the foregoing chapter has revealed discernible variations in the resource position and resource uses in different categories of sample milk suppliers in the two States. This may presumably also have an influence on the economics of dairy enterprise of the suppliers. The differences in the gross income derived from the dairying enterprise might be due to: (i) pattern of utilization of the resources and (ii) variations in the input uses and management practices. This chapter analyses the maintenance cost of rearing milch animals, cost of milk production and the pattern of income.

3.2 Definitional Aspects

For the cost analysis of milk production, concepts used in farm management studies have been adopted with suitable modifications. These are:

Cost A Includes all cash and kind expenses actually incurred by the milk suppliers such as feed, hired labour, interest on working capital, repairs and maintenance of equipments and veterinary charges.

Cost B Cost A + Interest on fixed capital.

Cost C Cost B+ Imputed value of family labour and home produced feed.

The following procedure was adopted for evaluating and apportioning of various costs:

(i) **Feed:** Data on feed provided by the sample dairy farmers to milch and other animals were collected in terms of both quantity and money (both dry and green). For evaluating the value of dry and green fodder from farm resources, the prevailing prices of purchased feed were used. Actual prices paid for feed concentrates only were taken into account.

(ii) **Depreciation:** No depreciation in the expenditure on the maintenance of milch animals and cost of milk production on account of milch animals, cattleshed, feeding troughs and dairy utensils. The rationale was that the value of milch animals appreciated during the initial period of rearing and depreciated only after the first calving. Similarly, cattleshed, feeding troughs and dairy utensils were also used for rearing other animals of the household and other household activities and it was difficult to apportion it to milch animals.

(iii) **Interest on Dairy Loans and other Fixed Assets:** The majority of the milk suppliers (borrowers)in the sample had borrowed from financial institutions. The amount of interest was accounted on the basis of actual interest paid on the amount outstanding during the year under reference. For investment in other fixed assets, including milch animals, interest was charged at 16 per cent per annum.

(iv) **Interest of Working Capital:** Interest on the working capital was on the estimated working capital during the reference year. The rate of interest charged was at the rate of 16 per cent per annum on the value of purchased items of food, grazing charges, repairs and maintenance expenses on cattleshed, troughs, dairy utensils and medicines.

(v) **Labour Charges:** The actual amount paid to the hired labour was accounted in this item of cost. The value of family labour was imputed at the prevailing wage rate in the villages for casual hired labour for different seasons and for males, females and children.

(vi) **Gross Income:** The gross income of the sample milk suppliers had accrued primarily from two sources: (i) milk production/sales and (ii) dung production. During the period of survey no sale of hide and skin was reported and income on account of sale of milch animals was restricted to one sample area in Gujarat. Since consumption of milk by the family members also constituted part of milk production, the average sale value of milk by the household was taken to be the estimated value of milk disposal. The actual sale value of milk by the dairy farmers was also discussed. Only the actual sale value of the products was considered for the quantity of milk converted into **mawa** and **ghee** by the households.

(vii) **Rearing:** Though rearing included all milch animals--dry as well as animals in milk and young stock--our analysis includes only adult milch animals. Similarly it would have been ideal to analyse costs and returns separately for cows and buffaloes, but owing to problems in data collection, the analysis refers to the mix of two.

3.3 Cost Structure

The various costs of maintenance of milch animals are presented in Table 3.1. There were significant differences between the member and non-member category of milk suppliers. Among the members, per-milch animal total cost (Cost C) was Rs. 15.34 per day in Gujarat and Rs. 17.30 per day in Maharashtra. Among the two regions the difference in the total cost for the member category of milk suppliers was to the extent of Rs. 1.96 per day in favour in Gujarat. Though a similar situation also existed for the non-members, the difference was lower as compared with members to the extert of Rs. 1.88 per day. The members incurred Rs. 8.69 per day as Cost A on the maintenance of milch animal in Gujarat as against Rs. 10.43 per day in Maharashtra. In the case of non-members, the cost was Rs. 9.38 and Rs. 10.81 per day for Gujarat and Maharashtra respectively.

The cooperative institutions in Gujarat and Maharashtra played a positive role in keeping the maintenance cost of milch animals low for the members. This was particularly reflected in Cost A. In Gujarat, the members had the better advantage of Re. 0.37 per day in Cost C as against Rs. 0.29 per day in Maharashtra. If Cost A is considered in the maintenance of milch animals, the Gujarat sample dairy farmers had a greater advantage through cooperatives.

TABLE 3.1 : Maintenance Cost per Milch Animal per Day for Different Categories of Milk Suppliers in Gujarat and Maharashtra.

(in Rs.)

Category of Milk Suppliers	Type	GUJARAT			MAHARASHTRA		
		Cost A	Cost B	Cost C	Cost A	Cost B	Cost C
Small	M	8.82	10.22	15.27	10.74	11.69	17.61
	NM	9.42	10.73	15.60	11.24	12.20	18.39
Medium	M	8.22	9.72	14.90	10.27	11.53	16.93
	NM	9.16	10.69	15.84	10.30	11.38	17.32
Big	M	8.20	9.82	14.62	10.28	11.65	16.69
	NM	9.42	10.57	16.08	-	-	-
Overall	M	8.69	10.22	15.34	10.43	11.62	17.30
	NM	9.38	10.75	15.71	10.81	11.83	17.59

Among different categories of milk suppliers, the total cost (Cost C) of maintenance of milch animals tended to decline with increase in the volume of milk supplies. This was observed in Gujarat and Maharashtra. The big category member milk suppliers had far greater advantages than non-members in the same category in Cost A. Per-milch animal maintenance Cost A was lower for members by Rs. 1.22 per day in the big category milk suppliers as against Rs. 0.60 per day in the small category in Gujarat. However, it is difficult to say about the prevailing situation in Maharashtra due to lack of comparable data of big category milk suppliers. But relatively, members had an advantage over non-members in the maintenance Cost A in small and medium categories of milk suppliers.

3.4 Cost Components

In view of the diversity in the maintenance cost between regions and the size of milk suppliers, the components of cost and their relative position are analysed (Tables 3.2 and 3.3).

Paid-out costs alone constituted 48.9 per cent and 51.5 per cent for members and non-members respectively in Gujarat. In Maharashtra they were 52 per cent for members and 53.1 per cent for non-members. This reveals two important aspects. Firstly, paid -out costs were higher in Maharashtra than in Gujarat. Secondly, members of the cooperatives had an advantage over non-members. Further, among different categories of milk suppliers, the proportion of paid-out costs tended to decline with increase in the supply of milk.

TABLE 3.2 : Components of Different Costs of Maintenance of Milch Animals in Different Categories of Milk Suppliers in Gujarat.

(fig. in %)

Items of Cost	Small		Medium		Big		Overall	
	M	NM	M	NM	M	NM	M	NM
Green & Dry Fodder	16.2	16.4	16.4	14.5	14.6	14.9	15.9	15.7
Oilcakes	5.4	5.9	3.6	4.7	5.6	5.9	5.0	5.5
Cottonseed & concentrates	23.2	27.8	23.4	23.1	24.2	25.4	22.9	27.1
Grazing & Labour charges	1.1	0.6	1.5	1.6	2.0	3.2	1.4	1.1
Medicines & Veterinary	3.5	1.7	2.5	1.5	1.8	0.9	2.4	1.7
expenses Others	0.4	0.6	0.2	0.5	0.3	0.2	0.3	0.4
TOTAL PAID-OUT COSTS	49.9	53.0	47.6	45.9	48.5	50.5	48.9	51.5
Interest on Working Capital	7.9	7.4	7.6	11.9	7.6	8.1	7.8	8.2
COST A	57.8	60.4	55.2	57.8	56.1	58.6	56.7	59.7
Interest on Investment of Milch animals	9.1	8.4	10.0	9.7	11.1	7.1	9.9	8.7
COST B	66.9	68.8	65.2	67.5	67.2	65.7	66.6	68.4
Imputed value of Home Produced Fodder	25.6	26.0	29.1	30.5	28.8	27.5	28.0	27.3
Imputed value of Family labour	7.5	5.2	5.7	2.0	4.0	6.8	5.4	4.3
COST C	100.0	100.0	100.0	100.0	100.0	100.0	100.0	100.0

Categories of Milk Suppliers: Small, Medium, Big, Overall.

M = Member NM = Non Member

Considering imputed costs, interest on working capital constituted about 8 per cent of of the total cost. The proportion of interest on milch animals varied among members and non-members and among regions. In Gujarat, it was about 9 per cent whereas it was around 6 per cent in Maharashtra. However, among imputed costs, the value of home-produced fodder was quite important and accounted for between 27 and 28 per cent in Gujarat and between 25 and 26 per cent in Maharashtra. Out-of-pocket expenses on fodder alone accounted for between 45 and 46 per cent in Maharashtra and about 44 per cent in Gujarat.

TABLE 3.3 : Components of Different Costs of Maintenance of Milch Animals in Different Categories of Milk Suppliers in Maharashtra.

(fig. in %)

Items of Cost	Categories of Milk Suppliers							
	Small		Medium		Big		Overall	
	M	NM	M	NM	M	NM	M	NM
Green & Dry Fodder	21.4	20.1	19.2	19.1	18.9	-	19.6	19.9
Oilcakes	7.4	7.0	7.8	9.3	8.7	-	7.9	8.2
Cottonseed & Concentrates	18.2	21.5	18.8	17.0	18.6	-	18.3	19.6
Grazing & Labour charges	0.1	0.2	0.1	-	0.2	-	0.2	0.2
Medicines & Veterinary expenses	0.6	0.5	1.7	0.8	1.9	-	1.3	0.8
Others	5.0	3.4	4.8	5.0	4.9	-	4.7	4.4
TOTAL PAID-OUT COSTS	52.7	52.7	52.4	51.3	53.2	-	52.0	53.1
Interest on Working Capital	8.3	8.4	8.3	8.2	8.4	-	8.3	8.4
COST A	61.0	61.1	60.7	59.5	61.6	-	60.3	61.5
Interest on Investment of Milch animals	5.4	5.2	7.4	6.2	8.2	-	6.9	5.8
COST B	66.4	66.3	68.1	65.7	69.8	-	67.2	67.3
Imputed value of Home Produced Fodder	26.8	24.8	25.1	27.9	25.4	-	26.5	25.0
Imputed value of family labour	6.8	8.9	6.8	6.4	4.8	-	6.3	7.7
COST C	100.0	100.0	100.	100.0	100.0	-	100.0	100.0

M = Member NM = Non Member

Inter-farm variations were also noticed among members and non-members in Maharashtra. This was particularly evident in paid-out costs which varied around 52 per cent of the total cost. However, variations were of more than 2 per cent among members and non-members and also among different categories of milk suppliers in Gujarat. In the paid-out cost, green and dry fodder, oilcakes and cottonseed and concentrates were the major items constituting about 44 per cent and 46 per cent for members in Gujarat and Maharashtra respectively. For non-members such costs accounted for about 48 per cent in Gujarat and Maharashtra. If the imputed cost of home-produced fodder was also added to the paid-out cost for purchased fodder, oilcakes and cottonseed and concentrates, it would amount to about three-fourths of the total cost. Feed costs might be a contributing factor in the milk pricing decisions and the total cost of milk production. It seems that farmers would be willing to take up dairying only if they could recover at least feed costs.

3.5 Cost of Milk Production

There are two schools of thought on the estimation of cost of milk production. One believes that adult milch animals have milk-yielding capabilities and expenditure on all these should be considered. The other school believes that only animals in milk should be considered since in the cost of cultivation of crops also only the area sown is considered. For our analysis, the cost of milk production has been estimated only for animals in milk.

It may be observed from Table 3.4 that the total cost (Cost C) of milk production per litre was less in Gujarat (Rs. 4.35) than in Maharashtra (Rs. 5.39) for the members of cooperatives. A similar situation also existed in respect of non-members as the cost was Rs. 6.32 per litre in Maharashtra and Rs. 4.48 per litre in Gujarat. The difference in the cost was quite high among members and non-members in Maharashtra than in Gujarat. The difference in the total cost was to the extent of Rs. 0.93 per litre for members in Maharashtra as against Rs. 0.13 for members in Gujarat. Paid-out costs were most important in influencing the total cost of milk production for both members and non-members.

Through cooperative efforts, members in Maharashtra had a greater advantage than in Gujarat in the cost of production. We have already seen the advantages in Cost C to the members of cooperatives in the previous paragraph and the advantage seems to be particularly on account of paid-out costs. In Maharashtra, members had the advantage to the extent of Rs. 0.55 per litre in the paid-out cost against Rs. 0.19 per litre in Gujarat.

Cost behaviour amongst the different categories of suppliers indicated operation of economies of scale. Total costs (Cost C) declined from Rs. 5.44 per litre to Rs. 3.19 per litre for members in Gujarat as one moved from small to big suppliers. Similarly in respect of non-members, per-litre total cost declined from Rs. 6 to Rs. 3.23. In Maharashtra, members and non-members gained in a similar manner. Among the members, big milk suppliers had the advantage of Rs. 1 per litre in Gujarat and Re. 0.78 per litre in Maharashtra in paid-out costs. This was also true of non-members. Though comparable data for non-members were not available in Maharashtra, big milk suppliers had an advantage to the extent of Rs. 1.53 per litre in Gujarat in respect of paid-out costs.

TABLE 3.4 : Per-Litre Cost of Milk Production in Different Categories of Milk Suppliers in Gujarat and Maharashtra.

Category of Milk Suppliers	Type	Per Litre Cost of Milk Production (in Rs.) GUJARAT Paid-out cost	Cost A	Cost B	Cost C	MAHARASHTRA Paid-out cost	Cost A	Cost B	Cost C
Small	M	2.53	3.14	3.64	5.44	3.28	3.80	4.14	6.24
	NM	3.18	3.62	4.13	6.00	3.51	4.07	4.41	6.65
Medium	M	2.23	2.48	3.06	4.69	2.70	3.13	3.52	5.16
	NM	2.69	3.12	3.64	5.39	3.17	3.68	4.06	6.18
Big	M	1.54	1.78	2.13	3.19	2.50	2.90	3.29	4.17
	NM	1.63	1.89	2.12	3.23	-	-	-	-
Overall	M	2.12	2.46	2.90	4.35	2.80	3.25	3.61	5.39
	NM	2.31	2.68	3.07	4.48	3.35	3.88	4.25	6.32

M = Member NM = Non-Member

3.6 Returns from Dairy Enterprise

Table 3.5 and 3.6 provide costs and returns on a per-milch-animal basis for the sample farmers in Gujarat and Maharashtra.

In both states, the sample farmers incurred losses if Cost C was taken into account. For the member category, farmers in Maharashtra incurred higher losses (Rs. 2,159 per milch animal) than those in Gujarat (Rs. 1,265). Net loss for non-members was Rs. 2,673 in Gujarat and Rs. 2,826 in Maharashtra. Big supplier members alone made a nominal profit of Rs. 46 per milch animal.

TABLE 3.5 : Differences in the value of Output per Milch Animal over Paid-out Costs, Cost A, B and C among Different Categories of Milk Suppliers in Gujarat.

(in Rs.)

Particulars	Small		Medium		Big		Overall	
	M	NM	M	NM	M	NM	M	NM
1. Gross Income	3302	2396	3823	4024	5382	5263	4334	3061
2. Paid-out Costs	2592	3019	2588	2884	2581	2964	2734	2933
3. Difference in Output Value over paid-out costs	710	-623	1235	1140	2801	2299	1600	108
4. COST A	3219	3438	2877	3343	2993	3438	3172	3424
5. Difference in output value over Cost A	83	-1042	746	681	2389	1825	1162	-363
6. COST B	3730	3916	3548	3902	3584	3858	3730	3924
7. Difference in output value over Cost B	-428	-1520	-275	122	1798	1405	604	-863
8. COST C	5574	5674	5439	5782	5336	5869	5599	5734
9. Difference in output value over Cost C	-2272	-3278	-1616	-1758	46	-606	-1265	-2673

Categories of Milk Suppliers: Small, Medium, Big, Overall.

M = Member NM = Non-Member

An examination of returns on the basis of paid-out costs, Cost A and Cost C indicated some distinct similarities and dissimilarities. First, members of cooperatives, on an average, could recover all cash expenses and items of interest on account of the working capital and investments in milch animals in Gujarat whereas in Maharashtra they were not able to recover expenditure on account of interest on investments, home-produced fodder and imputed value of family labour. However, in respect of non-members, returns were nominal to the extent of about Rs. 100 per milch animal after meeting only paid-out costs.

Second from among the different categories of sample milk suppliers, the small category of milk suppliers was put at the maximum disadvantage. Small milk suppliers particularly in Maharashtra incurred losses even after deducting only paid-out costs. This was applicable to both members and non-members. However, in Gujarat, members in the small category had an advantage of Rs. 710 per annum against a loss of Rs. 623 among non-members.

TABLE 3.6 : Differences in the value of Output Per Milch Animal over Paid-out Costs, Cost A, B and C among Different Categories of Milk Suppliers in Maharashtra.

(in Rs.)

Particulars	Small		Medium		Big		Overall	
	M	NM	M	NM	M	NM	M	NM
1. Gross Income	2745	2686	4298	4501	5303	-	4163	3594
2. Paid-out Costs	3380	3537	3234	3241	3238	-	3281	3402
3. Difference in Output Value over paid-out costs	-635	-851	1064	1260	2065	-	882	192
4. COST A	3920	4103	3749	3760	3752	-	3807	3946
5. Difference in output value over Cost A	-1175	-1417	549	741	1551	-	356	-352
6. COST B	4276	4453	4208	4154	4252	-	4241	4318
7. Difference in output value over Cost B	-1522	-1767	90	-347	1051	-	-78	-724
8. COST C	6428	6712	6179	6322	6092	-	6322	6420
9. Difference in output value over Cost C	-3683	-4026	-1881	-1821	-789	-	-2159	-2826

(Categories of Milk Suppliers: Small, Medium, Big, Overall)

M = Member NM = Non-Member

Third, big milk suppliers (members and non-members) in both states had the maximum income. In fact, big members had four times the income of the small category after meeting the paid-out costs.

This discussion is indicative of better management and better breeding practices followed by big dairy farmers. The prevailing situation demands greater attention by the cooperative institutions in particular to bring small milk suppliers near to the level of big suppliers. Attempts in this direction will sustain the long-term interest of small and medium size dairy farmers.

FOUR

UTILIZATION AND MARKETING OF MILK

4.1 Introduction

For a perishable commodity, such as milk, timely utilization and proper marketing at remunerative prices is as important as efforts to accelerate production and productivity. This chapter will examine domestic consumption of milk, its conversion into milk products and sales through different trade channels.

4.2 Utilization of Milk

It is of common knowledge that farm producers attempt to meet their consumption requirements of their daily necessities from their farm production. This can be applied to dairying activity also. However, the pattern of utilization of fluid milk produced by the sample dairy farmers suggested that in Gujarat domestic consumption (farm retention) among members and non-members was only 14.9 and 18.8 per cent respectively of the total milk production (Table 4.1). Relatively in Maharashtra, the proportion of domestic consumption of fluid milk was higher in both members and non-members than in Gujarat as it was 18.7 per cent in the former and 24 per cent in the latter category. Such a phenomenon of higher domestic consumption in Maharashtra was observed among members and non-members in different categories of milk suppliers. However, the proportion of home consumption of fluid milk to the total production was much higher in the small category milk suppliers than in the big suppliers in both categories of members and non-members. Among the member category of small milk suppliers, the consumption of fluid milk was 20.5 per cent of the total production in Gujarat and 31.4 per cent in Maharashtra. which declined to 11.4 per cent in the big category of Gujarat and 18.7 per cent in Maharashtra. Such

TABLE 4.1 : Utilization of Milk Production among Different Categories of Sample Milk Suppliers in Gujarat and Maharashtra.

(figs. in %)

Category of Milk Suppliers	Type	GUJARAT					MAHARASHTRA				
		Domestic consumption	Conversion into Ghee	Conversion into Mawa	Sales	Total	Domestic consumption	Conversion into Ghee	Conversion into Mawa	Sales	Total
Small	M	20.5	0.8	-	78.7	100.0	31.4	0.2	-	68.4	100.0
	NM	22.6	1.6	2.5	73.3	100.0	28.2	0.4	-	71.4	100.0
Medium	M	17.1	0.9	-	82.0	100.0	17.4	-	-	82.6	100.0
	NM	15.9	2.3	-	81.8	100.0	18.4	0.5	-	81.1	100.0
Big	M	11.4	3.0	1.0	84.6	100.0	18.7	0.1	-	81.2	100.0
	NM	11.4	7.7	-	80.9	100.0	-	-	-	-	-
Overall	M	14.9	1.9	0.5	82.7	100.0	18.7	0.1	-	81.2	100.0
	NM	18.8	2.4	1.3	77.5	100.0	24.0	0.4	-	75.6	100.0

Note: Domestic consumption also includes preparation of curd in the household and use of buttermilk prepared for domestic purposes and to give others along with food.

M = Member NM = Non-Member

wide differences were also observed in respect on non-members of different categories of milk suppliers.

It may further be observed from Table 4.1 that conversion of milk into ghee was to the extent of only about 2 per cent of the total production among members and 2.4 per cent in non-members in Gujarat. However, conversion of fluid milk for such purposes in Maharashtra was even less than in Gujarat and accounted for only 0.1 per cent among members and 0.4 per cent in non-members. Though conversion of fluid milk into ghee was at a very low level in Maharashtra, the big category of milk suppliers in Gujarat utilized a larger proportion of milk than small milk suppliers for conversion purposes. This was observed for both members and non-members in Gujarat.

Conversion of milk into **mawa** was virtually absent in Maharashtra. However, in Gujarat, about half per cent of the fluid milk disposals was converted into **mawa** by the members of cooperatives and 1.3 per cent by the non-members. Such a situation reflected that milk being a perishable commodity had a ready market for milk producers, and whatever was converted into products such as **mawa** was on account of seasonal changes in the requirements of urban population and the premium price available at a particular time of the season for such products.

Thus a substantial part of the total milk production was sold by the milk producers. In Gujarat, sample farmers in the member category sold a marginally higher proportion of fluid milk (82.7 per cent) than farmers of Maharashtra (81.2 per cent) in the same category. In respect of non-members also, sample dairy farmers in Gujarat had an advantage over their counterparts in Maharashtra. Among the different categories of milk suppliers, the proportion of sales of fluid milk logically increased with the increase in the supply of milk. However, the fact remains that more than 73 per cent of milk production was sold by the sample small farmers in Gujarat and they also tried to meet the nutritional requirements from milk for their family members.

4.3 Seasonal Changes in the Utilization of Milk

Generally food consumption patterns changed in the rural areas and it was hypothesized that utilization of fluid milk will also reflect seasonal changes. A detailed examination of prevailing conditions among sample farmers revealed some interesting features. First, sales of fluid milk were the lowest in winter and highest in the monsoons in both states (Tables 4.2 and 4.3). However, there were inter-farm variations in both states. Among small farmers, the proportion of sales of fluid milk was significantly lower among non-members than among members in all seasons. However, the difference in the proportion of sales of such farmers in Maharashtra was very marginal. Comparisons of sales of fluid milk indicated that the proportion of sales to the total disposals was substantially higher in Gujarat than in Maharashtra in all seasons. Among the medium and big farmers also the proportion of sale of fluid milk to the total was lower among non-members than among members.

Second, the conversion of fluid milk into ghee and **mawa** was relatively higher in winter than in monsoon and summer. Thus it appears that sales were affected in winter due to conversion. Among members, about 4 per cent of the total milk production in winter was converted into ghee and **mawa** in Gujarat as compared to about 2 per cent in monsoon and 1.5 per cent in summer. Conversion of fluid milk into ghee was undertaken on a very limited scale in Maharashtra, largely in monsoon.

Third, the consumption of fluid milk was highest in summer and lowest in monsoon for members in Gujarat. However, for non-members, the highest consumption was in winter and lowest in monsoon. Differences in the domestic consumption of fluid milk were quite marked among the members and non-members in Maharashtra. Highest consumption of fluid milk among the members was in winter and for non-members in monsoon. In Maharashtra highest variation in the consumption of milk was observed in monsoon among the members and non-members. Another important observation was that the domestic consumption of small milk suppliers was substantially higher than that of big farmers.

TABLE 4.2 : Seasonal Changes in the Utilization Pattern of Milk Production among Different Categories of Milk Suppliers in Gujarat.

(fig. in %)

Particulars	Category of Milk Suppliers							
	Small		Medium		Big		Overall	
	M	NM	M	NM	M	NM	M	NM
MONSOON								
Domestic Consumption	15.8	22.3	16.3	14.9	10.3	11.3	13.1	18.2
Conversion in to Ghee	0.4	-	1.2	2.8	2.1	4.7	1.5	1.5
Conversion in to Mawa	-	2.3	-	-	1.1	-	0.6	1.2
Sales	83.8	75.4	82.5	82.3	86.5	84.0	84.8	79.1
Total	100.0	100.0	100.0	100.0	100.0	100.0	100.0	100.0
WINTER								
Domestic Consumption	23.4	23.2	17.0	17.6	11.7	10.0	15.6	19.5
Conversion in to Ghee	1.3	3.5	1.3	3.1	5.0	11.8	3.2	4.4
Conversion in to Mawa	-	2.5	-	-	1.5	-	0.6	1.3
Sales	75.3	70.8	81.7	79.3	81.8	78.2	80.6	74.8
Total	100.0	100.0	100.0	100.0	100.0	100.0	100.0	100.0
SUMMER								
Domestic Consumption	24.7	23.1	18.3	15.2	12.6	13.6	16.4	18.6
Conversion in to Ghee	-	0.5	0.2	1.5	1.9	5.5	1.1	1.3
Conversion in to Mawa	-	2.9	-	-	0.9	-	0.4	1.4
Sales	75.3	73.5	81.5	83.3	84.6	80.9	82.1	78.7
Total	100.0	100.0	100.0	100.0	100.0	100.0	100.0	100.0

M = Member NM = Non-Member

In Gujarat, the extent of domestic utilization of fluid milk among the small category milk suppliers varied between 15.8 per cent in monsoon and 24.7 per cent in summer among the members as compared to between 10 per cent in winter and 13.6 per cent in summer among big farmers.

TABLE 4.3 : Seasonal Changes in the Utilization Pattern of Milk Production among Different Categories of sample Milk Suppliers in Maharashtra.

(fig. in %)

Particulars	Category of Milk Suppliers							
	Small		Medium		Big		Overall	
	NM	M	NM	M	NM	M	NM	
MONSOON								
Domestic Consumption	32.8	31.2	17.0	23.1	17.1	-	17.1	26.5
Conversion in to Ghee	0.7	2.2	-	0.8	0.1	-	0.1	1.4
Conversion in to Mawa	-	-	-	-	-	-	-	-
Sales	66.5	66.6	83.0	76.1	82.8	-	82.8	72.1
Total	100.0	100.0	100.0	100.0	100.0	-	100.0	100.0
WINTER								
Domestic Consumption	30.1	29.8	22.4	16.6	21.7	-	21.7	24.4
Conversion in to Ghee	-	-	-	0.6	-	-	-	0.2
Conversion in to Mawa	-	-	-	-	-	-	-	-
Sales	69.9	70.2	77.6	82.8	78.3	-	78.3	75.4
Total	100.0	100.0	100.0	100.0	100.0	-	100.0	100.0
SUMMER								
Domestic Consumption	31.3	25.8	13.8	15.8	17.4	-	17.4	22.1
Conversion in to Ghee	0.3	-	-	0.2	0.2	-	0.2	0.1
Conversion in to Mawa	-	-	-	-	-	-	-	-
Sales	68.4	74.2	86.2	84.0	82.4	-	82.4	77.8
Total	100.0	100.0	100.0	100.0	100.0	-	100.0	100.0

M = Member MM = Non-Member

4.4 Per Capita Domestic Consumption of Fluid Milk

Among different regions of the country, per capita availability of milk in 1981 was the highest (203.63 g) in the northern region, followed by the western region (125.53 g), southern region (96.32 g), central region (88.02 g) and eastern region (73.15 g).[1] The National

1. *Indian Dairy Year Book*, 1983, p. 64.

Advisory Committee of the Indian Council of Medical Research has favoured a minimum requirement of 284 g per capita per day for a balanced diet.

Keeping in view both the norms of comparison, it was observed that the per capita milk consumption was much less than the nutritional requirements among the sample farmers in both States (Table 4.4). In Gujarat, the per capita consumption of milk varied between 197 g per day among the members and 204 g among the non-members. The Per capita consumption among the members was a little higher in Maharashtra (215 g) than in Gujarat.[2] However, non-members in Gujarat had a significantly higher per capita milk consumption (204 g) per day than that of the same category in Maharashtra (137 g). It is important to note this was so in spite of the fact that the marketed surplus in Gujarat was much higher as compared to Maharashtra in the non-member category of milk suppliers.

The seasonal pattern of milk consumption indicated that the per capita per-day milk consumption was highest in winter and lowest in summer among the members of cooperatives. Though a similar pattern was observed among the non-members in Gujarat, sample farmers in Maharashtra showed lowest consumption in the mansoon season.

Among the different categories of milk suppliers, with the exception of the big category milk suppliers in Maharashtra, all member and non-member categories consumed milk much below the level of nutritional requirements. However the small category milk suppliers were at the greatest disadvantage as compared to medium and big categories. In fact the per capita consumption of milk per day among the small category was about half that of the big category milk suppliers in both states.

---

2. Per capita milk consumption was estimated on the basis of consumption units in the family. The units were calculated thus: Male-1.0, above 18 years; Female-0.9 above 18 years; Male-0.8, between 16-18 years; Female-0.8, between 16-18 years; Male and Female-0.7, below 16 years.

TABLE 4.4 : Per Capita Domestic Consumption of Milk per day among Different Categories of Sample Milk Suppliers in Gujarat and Maharashtra

(fig. in %)

State	Season	Small		Medium		Big		Overall	
		M	NM	M	NM	M	NM	M	NM
GUJARAT									
	Monsoon	125	199	215	219	270	109	198	219
	Winter	156	192	220	232	266	109	210	221
	Summer	121	136	198	199	243	109	183	171
	Overall	134	172	211	217	260	109	197	204
MAHARASHTRA									
	Monsoon	133	72	205	220	303	-	198	109
	Winter	143	138	285	159	361	-	237	143
	Summer	157	156	214	168	295	-	209	159
	Overall	144	122	285	182	320	-	215	137

But it seems that the per capita consumption of milk per day among the sample milk producers was substantially higher than the State averages estimated by the Operations Research Group (ORG), Baroda. According to ORG estimates, per capita consumption of milk per day was 132 g in Gujarat and 89 g in Maharashtra.[3]

Although the per capita consumption of fluid milk per day was much lower than the nutritional requirement it was much higher than the average availability of milk for consumption in the western region amongst all the classes of milk producers. It may be stated that particularly small farmers sacrificed their milk needs in a much higher proportion than the medium and big category farmers when compared to the minimum requirement of 284 g. This was applicable for the sample farmers of both States. It seems that small farmers in both States in the member categories found a ready market for milk in the organized dairy sector and preferred to sell it to meet other household requirements. Therefore, they consumed less milk on a per capita basis as compared to other categories of milk suppliers.

---

3. Food Habit Survey conducted by the Operations Research Group, Baroda. Quoted from the paper on some questions concerning milk in Operation Flood Project by Dilip Shah, presented at UGC sponsored Regional Seminar on Milk Pricing and Marketing Practices held at Surat on January 4-5, 1984.

4.5 Marketable and Marketed Surplus of Milk

It may be mentioned first that in the estimation of the marketable surplus of milk, only domestic consumption requirements based on nutritional recommendations were considered. The rationale was that milk being a perishable commodity was not bartered for services hired. Further, it had to be disposed within a short duration to avoid souring.

It may be observed from Table 4.5 that the marketable surplus of milk among the sample dairy farmers in Gujarat was 78.2 per cent among members and 73.2 per cent among non-members. A higher marketable surplus among members than non-members was also observed in Maharashtra. But the proportion of the marketable surplus among non-members in Maharashtra was significantly less (49.4 per cent of the total milk production) than that among members (74.9 per cent). In Gujarat also the marketable surplus among members was higher by about 5 per cent than among non-members. The implication is that organization of milk collection by the cooperative dairy in both States has encouraged milk producers of all categories to increase milk production and consequently the marketable surplus. This contention was also supported by the extent of marketable surplus of different categories of milk supplies in the sample of both States. Although the marketable surplus of milk among the big category members of cooperatives was to the extent of 87.2 per cent and 86.7 per cent in Gujarat and Maharashtra respectively, small farmers were also not lagging behind.Though the small category milk suppliers in the member category in Maharashtra had a smaller marketable surplus of milk (37.4 per cent), the extent of the marketable surplus of the small category in Gujarat was to the extent of 55.8 per cent of the total milk production. In respect of non-members also, the marketabl surplus in the small category milk supplier was about 70 per cent of the total milk production and matched with the marketable surplus of the big category suppliers. Similarly the marketable surplus of milk among the non-members in Maharashtra was one-third of the total milk production in the small category and as high as 71 per cent among the medium category.

Table 4.5 : Marketable and Marketed Surplus of Milk among Different Categories of Milk Suppliers in Different Seasons in Gujarat and Maharashtra.

(Fig.in %)

State	Category of Milk Suppliers	Type	Monsoon		Winter		Summer		Overall	
			% of marketable surplus to production	% of marketed surplus to production	% of marketable surplus to production	% of marketed surplus to production	% of marketable surplus to production	% of marketed surplus to production	% of marketable surplus to production	% of marketed surplus to production
GUJARAT										
	Small	M	63.6	83.8	56.6	75.3	42.4	75.8	55.8	78.7
		NM	74.3	75.4	71.4	70.8	61.0	73.5	69.8	72.3
	Medium	M	78.1	82.5	77.6	81.7	73.2	81.5	76.5	82.0
		NM	80.2	82.3	78.0	79.3	78.0	83.3	78.8	81.8
	Big	M	88.9	86.5	87.2	81.8	84.9	84.6	87.2	84.6
		NM	69.8	84.0	73.8	78.2	63.8	80.9	69.7	80.9
	Overall	M	80.8	84.8	78.6	80.6	74.1	82.1	78.2	82.7
		NM	76.0	79.1	74.0	74.8	68.6	78.7	73.2	77.5
MAHARASHTRA										
	Small	M	28.9	66.5	39.3	69.9	42.3	68.4	37.4	68.4
		NM	24.7	66.6	37.6	70.2	52.3	74.2	33.3	71.4
	Medium	M	76.1	83.0	77.2	77.6	81.5	86.2	78.6	82.6
		NM	69.7	76.1	69.8	82.8	72.9	84.0	70.9	81.1
	Big	M	88.0	82.8	85.3	78.3	86.6	82.4	86.7	81.2
		NM	-	-	-	-	-	-	-	-
	Overall	M	75.1	82.8	73.3	78.3	76.0	82.4	74.9	81.2
		NM	29.5	72.1	50.7	75.4	59.8	77.8	49.4	75.6

M = Member NM = Non-Member

Further examination of the marketable surplus of milk in different seasons revealed that the proportion was highest in monsoon and lowest in summer. This was observed in the case of both members and non-members in Gujarat. However, in Maharashtra, the marketable surplus of milk was less in monsoon than in summer among both members and non-members and this was perhaps due to the lactation period of the milch animals.

There were also similarities and dissimilarities in the marketable surplus of milk in different seasons particularly for small farmers. In summer, the proportion of the marketable surplus of milk for members was almost equal in Gujarat and Maharashtra among small farmers whereas in respect of non-members it was higher by about 8 per cent in Gujarat than in Maharashtra. In monsoon and winter, the proportion of the marketable surplus of small dairy farmers both in member and non-member categories was higher in Gujarat than in Maharashtra. However, in the medium and big category milk supplies, the proportion of marketable surplus to total production was more than three:four in Gujarat and Maharashtra.

As against the potential marketable surplus, the marketed surplus was higher among the sample dairy farmers in both States. In fact, the marketed surplus was higher than the marketable surplus by about 4 per cent among members and non-members in Gujarat. In Maharashtra, the marketed surplus was higher than the marketable surplus by 6 per cent among members and by about 25 per cent among non-members. This situation was also observed among different categories of milk suppliers with the exception of big categories of member suppliers. However, the highest difference between marketable and marketed surplus was in the small category milk suppliers. Small milk suppliers in the member category marketed about 23 per cent more than their marketable surplus in Gujarat and about 31 per cent in Maharashtra. Though among non-members the difference was of only about 2 per cent, in Maharashtra the surplus was about 28 per cent. Again, among the different categories of sample milk suppliers, only the small showed a large variation in marketed surplus and marketable surplus in all three seasons. Among the members the difference in marketed surplus and marketable surplus was 20 per cent in monsoon, 19 per cent in winter and 33 per cent in summer in favour of the former in

Gujarat. Such differences, of higher marketed surplus than marketable, were to the extent of 41 per cent in monsoon season, 32 per cent in winter season and 22 per cent in summer season in Maharashtra. However, the differences were very marginal in Gujarat. Also, in the medium and big category suppliers, both members and non-members, differences between marketable and marketed surplus were marginal.

4.6 Agencies of Sales of Milk

For the sake of convenience to clearly understand the role of cooperatives to mop up the marketed surplus of milk, different agencies to whom sales were effected by the sample milk producers were clubbed into three categories. They are organized cooperative milk societies, private vendors and others engaged in direct sales of milk to consumers and sweets merchants in nearby urban areas and within the villages. Agencywise proportion of sales in different seasons is presented in Tables 4.6 and 4.7.

About 99 per cent of the total sales were made by the sample dairy farmers to their cooperative organizations in both States. The share of private vendors was 0.8 per cent in Gujarat and 0.4 per cent in Maharashtra. Direct sales by members to consumers and urban consumers and merchants were merely 0.1 per cent in Gujarat and Maharashtra.

In respect of non-members, in Gujarat about 62 per cent of the total sales were direct to urban consumers and sweets merchants in comparison to less than 1 per cent in Maharashtra. Private vendors' share in the total sales was about 13 per cent in Gujarat and 22 per cent in Maharashtra. Despite being non-members, sales of marketed surplus of milk to the cooperative dairy were to the extent of 25 per cent in Gujarati and 717 per cent in Maharashtra. It may be pointed out that payment to milk suppliers by the primary village cooperatives was sometimes weekly on the basis of quality consideration, whereas private trade made payment in advance which was generally much less than the ruling marketing price.

Table 4.6 : Agencywise Seasonal Sales of Fluid Milk among Different Categories of Sample Milk Suppliers in Gujarat.

(Fig. in %)

Categories of milk suppli-ers	Type	Seasons and Agencies															
		Monsoon				Winter				Summer				Overall			
		Milk Coop.	Du-dhias	Oth-ers	Total	Milk Coop.	Du-dhias	Oth-ers	Total	Milk Coop.	Du-dhias	Oth-ers	Total	Milk Coop.	Du-dhias	Oth-ers	Total
Small	M	95.6	4.4	-	100.0	100.0	-	-	100.0	100.0	-	-	100.0	98.1	1.9	-	100.0
	NM	36.3	12.5	51.2	100.0	59.8	7.4	32.8	100.0	60.0	-	40.0	100.0	50.4	7.6	42.0	100.0
Medium	M	95.7	3.3	1.00	100.0	100.0	-	-	100.0	99.2	0.8	-	100.0	98.2	1.4	0.4	100.0
	NM	-	26.9	73.1	100.0	-	27.9	72.1	100.0	8.9	12.8	78.3	100.0	3.0	22.5	74.5	100.0
Big	M	100.0	-	-	100.0	100.0	-	-	100.0	100.0	-	-	100.0	100.0	-	-	100.0
	NM	-	-	100.0	100.0	-	-	100.0	100.0	-	-	100.0	100.0	-	-	100.0	100.0
Overall	M	97.9	1.8	0.3	100.0	100.0	-	-	100.0	99.7	0.3	-	100.0	99.1	0.8	0.1	100.0
	NM	18.1	16.1	65.3	100.0	29.2	14.0	56.0	100.0	29.3	5.8	64.9	100.0	25.1	12.6	62.3	100.0

M = Member NM = Non-Member

Table 4.7 : Agencywise Seasonal Sales of Fluid Milk among Different Categories of Sample Milk Suppliers in Maharashtra.

(Fig. in %)

Categories of milk suppliers	Type	Monsoon				Winter				Summer				Overall			
		Milk Coop.	Dudhias	Others	Total	Milk Coop.	Dudhias	Others	Total	Milk Coop.	Dudhias	Others	Total	Milk Coop.	Dudhias	Others	Total
Small	M	99.1	0.9	-	100.0	100.0	-	-	100.0	96.1	3.7	0.2	100.0	98.3	1.6	0.1	100.0
	NM	95.0	5.0	-	100.0	82.1	17.9	-	100.0	80.2	19.8	-	100.0	83.3	16.7	-	100.0
Medium	M	100.0	-	-	100.0	98.1	1.9	-	100.0	100.0	-	-	100.0	99.4	0.6	-	100.0
	NM	100.0	-	-	100.0	55.6	44.4	-	100.0	59.8	35.8	4.4	100.0	70.5	27.9	1.6	100.0
Big	M	100.0	-	-	100.0	100.0	-	-	100.0	100.0	-	-	100.0	100.0	-	-	100.0
	NM	-	-	-	-	-	-	-	-	-	-	-	-	-	-	-	-
Overall	M	99.9	0.1	-	100.0	99.5	0.5	-	100.0	99.3	0.6	0.1	100.0	99.5	0.4	0.1	100.0
	NM	98.0	2.0	-	100.0	70.3	29.7	-	100.0	72.1	26.1	1.8	100.0	77.4	21.8	0.8	100.0

M = Member NM = Non=Member

However, interfarm and interregion differences were observed among both members and non-members. The big category member milk suppliers both in Gujarat and Maharashtra marketed only to the cooperatives. In respect of the small and medium category, sales were about 98 per cent of the total sales in both States. Among non-members, more than 75 per cent of the total sales were to urban merchants and direct consumers in the medium and big category milk suppliers in Gujarat but in the small category milk suppliers, about 50 per cent of the total sales were to the cooperatives. In Maharashtra also, sales to cooperatives by small and medium categories of milk suppliers were 83.3 and 70.5 per cent of the total respectively.

If the seasonal pattern of sales was considered, of the cooperatives were more than 98 per cent of the total sales of the members to the cooperative dairy organization in both States. But non-members showed variations and sales to the cooperative dairy were higher in winter and summer than in monsoon in Gujarat. In Maharashtra, highest sales to cooperatives by non-members were in monsoon and lowest in summer. Thus, it appears that farmers in the non-member category tried to take advantage of the cooperative structure according to their convenience in terms of the possibility of obtaining a better price and capacity of the private trade to utilize their disposable milk surplus.

4.7 Average Price Realizations

In view of multiplicity of agencies involved in procuring milk from the producers, agencywise price realizations by the sample milk producers have been classified into two broad categories. They are milk cooperatives and other agencies. Agencywise seasonal variations in the prices realized through sale of fluid milk by the sample milk producers is presented in Table 4.8.

It was observed that in Gujarat, among members, sales to other private agencies on an average realized a better price than sales to dairy cooperatives. As against the average price of Rs.3.20 per litre by sales to the cooperative dairies, realization per litre was Rs.3.28 by sales to the private trade. A similar situation was also observed among non-members also where the difference was to the extent of

Table 4.8 : Agencywise Seasonal Average Price Realization among Different Categories of Sample Milk Suppliers in Gujarat and Maharashtra.

(in Rs. per litre)

Category of milk suppliers	Type	GUJARAT Monsoon Dairy	Monsoon Others	Winter Dairy	Winter Others	Summer Dairy	Summer Others	Overall Dairy	Overall Others	MAHARASHTRA Monsoon Dairy	Monsoon Others	Winter Dairy	Winter Others	Summer Dairy	Summer Others	Overall Dairy	Overall Others
Small	M	2.43	3.10	3.30	-	3.35	-	2.94	3.10	2.82	3.50	3.11	-	3.07	3.50	3.01	3.50
	NM	2.80	3.08	2.39	2.99	3.03	3.05	2.70	3.05	2.27	3.20	2.80	3.32	3.12	3.56	2.85	3.46
Medium	M	2.89	3.45	3.02	-	3.19	3.00	3.03	3.39	2.49	-	2.85	2.15	2.81	-	2.75	2.15
	NM	-	3.30	-	3.42	3.00	3.50	3.00	3.40	-	2.84	-	2.69	3.35	2.97	3.28	3.31
Big	M	3.11	-	3.61	-	3.47	-	3.37	nil	2.54	-	2.70	-	2.81	-	2.68	-
	NM	-	3.89	-	3.92	-	3.91	-	3.91	-	-	-	-	-	-	-	-
Overall	M	2.92	3.30	3.37	-	3.37	3.00	3.20	3.28	2.57	3.50	2.81	2.15	2.85	3.50	2.74	2.53
	NM	2.80	3.30	2.39	3.40	3.03	3.46	2.72	3.38	2.63	3.20	2.76	3.34	3.07	3.40	2.85	3.37

M = Member NM = Non-Member

Rs.0.66 per litre in favour of the private trade. However, in Maharashtra, members of cooperatives realized better prices of milk through sales to cooperatives (Rs.2.74 per litre) than to the private trade (Rs.2.53 per litre). As in the case of Gujarat, non-members in Maharashtra also realized better prices through sales to the private trade than to cooperatives and the difference was to the extent of Rs.0.52 per litre in favour of the private trade.

Among the different categories of milk suppliers in Gujarat, the average price realisation per litre was higher for the big suppliers, from the other categories. It can be observed from table 4.8 that Average realisation per litre of milk tend to increase with the quantum of supplies. This is irrespective of the agency through which the producer has disposed of milk and the same is applicable for members as well as non-members. However, in Maharashtra, average price realisation per litre was highest among small category of milk suppliers of both members and non-members through sales to Cooperatives, than medium and big categories of milk suppliers.

The average price per litre realized was significantly higher in monsoon and summer in Gujarat and cooperatives offered nearly the same as the private trade in this season. It was important to note that non-members realized lower prices through sales to the cooperative dairy in all three seasons than what they received from the private trade despite the fact that they marketed about 25 per cent of their total production to the cooperatives.

In Maharashtra also, with the exception of the winter season, the sample milk producers realized better prices through sales to private trade agencies than to cooperatives in all the three seasons. The difference in the price of milk offered by the private trade the milk cooperatives was much higher in all seasons among non-members.Despite price disadvantages through sales to cooperatives, the sample non-member farmers sold 77 per cent of their surplus the cooperatives.

FIVE

COOPERATIVE MILK PROCUREMENT, PROCESSING AND MARKETING

5.1 **Introduction**

This chapter examines two typical situations–the fully integrated approach which is operative in Gujarat and the marginal integrative approach in Maharashtra.

Three milk unions in Gujarat were selected: Sagar Union at Mehsana, Sumul Union at Surat and Sabar Union at Sabarkantha.[1] The unions were linked with specialized village level milk societies engaged singly in the distribution of cattle feed for milch animals and collection of milk. They also had their own cattle feed manufacturing plants. In Maharashtra also, three unions were selected: Krishna Milk Supply Union at Miraj, Hanuman Milk Supply Union at Yelguda and Warananagar Union at Amritnagar. The first two were primarily engaged in milk collection within Sangli district and supplying milk to the processing plant located at Miraj which, in turn, worked as a feeder unit for the Bombay Milk Supply Scheme. The Warananagar Union collected milk from the adjoining area within its jurisdiction and worked also as a feeder unit. About 90 per cent of its total milk collection was supplied to the Kolhapur District Supply Union and the remaining converted into products such as **peda, srikhand** and **gulab jamun** for local sale. This Union had earlier functioned as an exclusive feeder unit but now owned a processing plant. However, a large part of the milk collected through the cooperatives was chilled and transported to Bombay and only a small part was converted into milk powder and butter for sale in local areas. It is important to mention here that the three selected milk

---

1. The unions are better known by the brand names of their products.

unions in Maharashtra were established as part of the development programmes of the sugar cooperatives. In the first instance, milk collection was done by the same village cooperatives which were engaged in the distribution of credit and other agro-inputs (multipurpose societies). Warananagar later developed village level milk cooperatives. Yelguda still does not have a primary milk producers cooperative. Comparable data from the selected primaries of Warananagar and Miraj were not available. Therefore, the performance of the village cooperatives was not studied in detail in Maharashtra, and the presentation in the following sub-sections refers only to the five primary village cooperatives in the area of operation of each of the three selected unions in Gujarat which specialized in the business and were procuring milk from the surveyed farm households engaged in dairying in such primaries. The analysis in the following sub-sections is based on published data available up to 1980-81. It must be noted that such data was not available for 1981-82 at the time of survey, and as such comparisons with the cost and return analysis based on farmer data in the earlier chapters were not possible. However, the costs and returns can be usefully compared between Gujarat and Maharashtra.

5.2 Performance of Village Cooperatives

5.2.1 Coverage of Membership

It may be mentioned that the selected dairy unions in Gujarat were established long ago over the years these have developed a broad-based organizational structure to market milk. An examination of the coverage of membership of milk producers revealed that during the period 1976-77 to 1980-81, per-society number of members did not show an appreciable increase in the jurisdiction of all the three selected dairy unions. In fact, there was a decrease in the villages under the jurisdiction of the Sumul Dairy. One of the highlights of the membership pattern was that the number almost remained static in the jurisdiction of the Sagar Dairy, while there was some increase in the membership per society under the jurisdiction of the Sabar Dairy union. The details of the coverage of the membership under the jurisdiction of each selected dairy unit are presented in Table.

TABLE 5.1 : Coverage of Membership and Per-Member Milk Procurement by the Selected Village Level Cooperatives under the Jurisdiction of Selected Dairies in Gujarat, 1976-77 to 1980-81.

Year	Coverage of Membership			Milk procurement per Member (litres)		
	Sagar Dairy	Sumul Dairy	Sabar Dairy	Sagar Dairy	Sumul Dairy	Sabar Dairy
1976-77	180	183	89	818	502	765
1977-78	166	164	79	1001	521	956
1978-79	180	153	120	830	506	720
1979-80	208	140	118	803	570	743
1980-81	180	138	109	946	486	776

5.2.2. Milk Procurement

In 1980-81, each member in the village supplied on an average 946 litres of milk during the cooperative year to the village society in the jurisdiction of the Sagar Dairy area. The corresponding quantities for the Sabar and Sumul dairies were 776 litres and 486 litres respectively. Further the trend indicated that there was little increase in the supply of milk per member. Further, milk disposals by the members also depended on the domestic consumption requirements and available prices in other market channels. The dairies have realized the fact that any increase in milk procurement per member can now be through efforts in increasing the productivity of milch animals. Therefore, it augurs well for the investment made by the cooperatives for enhancing milk production.

5.2.3. System of Procurement, Pricing and Payments

We will now examine the system of procurement followed by village cooperatives and the pricing and payment schedules. Each society had specified a time in the morning and evening for delivery of milk. Milk being a highly perishable commodity required planned flow from the producer to the dairy plant dock of the union in view of the vast stretches of the area covered by the processing unit and the seasonal changes in temperature. Village level cooperatives have provided a Pass Book to each member of the cooperative wherein entries are made by the society official at the time of delivery of milk about the quantity of milk, butter fat content and the value of the milk. The payable amount of the yearly bonus was calculated at the end of the year on the basis of the monthly entries in the Pass Book.

The quality of milk was considered to be of prime importance and the fat content of the milk was taken as the basis. Milk testing was done at the village society level by the tester of the society. Since milk producers also reared cows, the pricing system took into account both fat content and solids not fat. Milk producer members of the society receive part payment based on the provisional price of milk delivered to the society every twelve hours, round the year.

5.2.4 Milk Business Transactions by the Societies

Along with the milk procurement and adoption of a system to fix the price and payment schedule, it is also important to understand the share of price realizations by the producers and the society. It may again be mentioned that apart from the year-round value of milk supplied to the society, a member producer also receives bonus and dividend from the profits of the society at the end of the year. Also the society incurs some expenditure on account of wages, salaries, society office maintenance, etc. Since milk collection was the main activity and since it was difficult to apportion expenses on the three activities undertaken by the society, the cost of handling and net profit estimates should be interpreted keeping these factors in view. Data on the payments made to the member milk suppliers, realizations from the sales of milk to the milk processing union and accrued net profits for the surveyed village level societies are presented in Table 5.2. The figures are averages for the selected village cooperatives in the jurisdiction of the dairy union. Since the surveyed village level cooperatives have supplied the maximum quantity of milk on the route of one direction, it is presumed that they were best in this performance and generalizations based on these should be interpreted with caution.

Among the selected village cooperatives, wide differences were observed in the payment of milk price to the member producers. Such differences were also observed over the period. It is interesting to observe that in 1980-81, the village societies paid Rs: 232.20 per 100 litres of milk in the jurisdiction of the Sumul Dairy and Rs. 200.62 per 100 litres in the Sagar Dairy area.

Table 5.2 : Sales Realization, Prices Received by the Milk Producers, Cost of Handling and Net Profits accrued by to Village Level Cooperatives under the Jurisdiction of Selected Dairy Unions in Gujarat, 1976-77 to 1980-81.

(in Rs. per 100 litres)

Societies in the jurisdiction of	Year	Realization from sales of milk by the society from union	Price Paid to milk Producers: Final price and Bonus	Divi-dend	Total	Difference in the price realized by the society and paid to the farmer	Cost of milk handling at the society level	Net profit accrued per society
Sagar	1976-77	171.71	169.26	0.28	169.54	2.17	1.70	49398
	1977-78	181.91	178.25	0.30	178.55	3.36	2.09	52889
	1978-79	192.60	187.77	0.34	188.11	4.49	2.18	49886
	1979-80	198.91	190.51	0.32	190.83	8.08	3.26	61326
	1980-81	216.38	200.32	0.30	200.62	15.76	3.36	84316
Sabar	1976-77	178.36	172.38	0.28	173.61	4.75	3.12	23561
	1977-78	186.20	173.99	0.26	174.25	11.95	3.62	27857
	1978-79	184.34	176.04	0.20	176.24	12.10	3.85	27381
	1979-80	192.30	182.83	0.20	183.03	9.27	3.98	30498
	1980-81	219.54	213.31	0.25	213.56	5.98	4.03	41185
Sumul	1976-77	N.A.	N.A.	N.A.	N.A.	N.A.	N.A.	N.A.
	1977-78	N.A.	N.A.	N.A.	N.A.	N.A.	N.A.	N.A.
	1978-79	229.00	216.00	0.18	216.18	12.82	3.08	2907
	1979-80	216.00	207.00	0.23	207.23	8.77	3.17	7952
	1980-81	243.00	232.00	0.20	232.20	10.80	3.46	8639

N.A. = Not Available.

The amount included the final price, bonus and dividend paid to the member milk producers. Figures for this amount from 1976-77 to 1980-81 revealed that the value of milk per 100 litres showed a steady increase over the period. This was also true in the case of the selected village cooperatives of all the three dairy unions. The differences in the prices could be observed from the fact that for the Sagar Dairy village societies, the minimum and maximum range of milk price paid was between Rs. 169 and Rs. 201 per 100 litres between 1976-77 and 1980-81: However, the minimum price paid by the Sabar and Sumul dairy village cooperatives during the period under reference was higher than the Sagar Dairy village cooperatives. For the Sabar Dairy villages the minimum price was Rs.174.00 per 100 litres and for Sumul it was Rs. 207.00 per 100 litres. Similarly the maximum price paid by the village societies was the highest (Rs. 232.20 per 100 litres) for the Sumul Dairy societies; it was Rs. 214 per 100 litres for the Sabar and only Rs. 201 per 100 litres for the Sagar Dairy societies. It must be noted that societies in the Sagar area accepted cow milk in all the years under reference, while societies in the Sabar and Sumul areas accepted only buffalo milk. This may be the reason for lower realizations per 100 litres in the Sagar area.

Since the price of milk paid to producer members was on the basis of the price received by the society from the dairy (which was based on the fat content), such differences in the maximum and minimum prices during the period 1976-77 to 1980-81 were observed also in the value realized by the societies. The societies also incur expenditure on the handling of milk, distribution of feed to members and sale of products of the dairy. Such costs showed an increase during the period under reference. However, village level cooperatives in the Sagar Dairy area showed lower handling costs.

An important aspect was of increasing retention of money surplus of the business by the societies. After incurring handling expenses, societies in the Sagar Dairy area had a larger surplus than the societies in the Sabar and Sumul regions. On the basis of surplus in the milk business and other incomes from sales of feed, etc., societies in the Sagar Dairy region were at an advantage. This can also be substantiated from the yearly net profits accrued to societies. It may be observed that the yearly net profits of the village level societies increased from Rs. 49.000 in 1976-77 to Rs. 84,000 in 1980-81 for the societies in the area of the Sagar Dairy and from Rs. 23,000 to Rs. 41,000 in the Sabar Dairy area. However, societies in the jurisdiction of the Sumul Dairy had the smallest net profits although these increased from Rs. 2,900 in 1978-79 to Rs. 8,600 in 1980-81.

Retentions of net profits with the village milk cooperative societies have in fact contributed to their increasing owned funds (Table 5.3). Owned funds comprising share capital, reserve and other funds increased from Rs. 1.53 lakh in 1976-77 to Rs. 4.16 lakh in 1980-81 for the village societies in the Sagar Dairy area. The increase in the owned funds was, on an average, about 35 per cent per year for the societies in the Sagar Dairy area; societies of the Sabar Dairy area had a similar increase. Total owned capital for the societies in the Sabar Dairy area increased from Rs. 1.11 lakh in 1976-77 to Rs. 2.85 lakh in 1980-81. But the village societies in the Sumul Dairy area did not increase owned funds in the same proportion as societies in the Sagar and Sabar dairy areas. This may also be a reason for it not to be able to pay to the milk producers higher prices compared to societies in the Sagar and Sabar Dairy areas. On the whole, it may be noted that in the case of village societies under selected dairy units owned funds more than doubled during the five-year period.

Table 5.3 : Progress of Capital Formation of Village Level Milk Cooperatives under the Jurisdiction of Selected Dairy Units in Gujarat, 1976-77 to 1980-81.

Societies in jurisdiction of	Year	Equity				Percentage increase of total funds over 1976-77 = 100.00
		Share Capital (Rs.)	Reserve Funds (Rs.)	Other Funds (Rs.)	Total	
Sagar	1976-77	44996	44554	61163	153713	100.00
	1977-78	45746	60776	100830	207352	134.90
	1978-79	52087	73247	138244	263578	171.47
	1979-80	52217	88579	184238	325034	211.46
	1980-81	59232	109658	247475	416365	270.87
Sabar	1976-77	57813	13960	39646	111419	100.00
	1977-78	110370	20924	60539	191833	172.17
	1978-79	110752	27769	81075	219596	197.09
	1979-80	101326	35394	103948	240668	216.00
	1980-81	105192	45690	134837	285719	256.44
Sumul	1976-77	8360	10360	5421	24141	100.00
	1977-78	9740	12578	8621	30939	128.16
	1978-79	10740	13305	10801	34846	144.34
	1979-80	12437	15293	16765	44495	184.31
	1980-81	14430	17453	23244	55127	228.35

* other funds consist of buildings, education, dividend equalization, etc.

A few issues emerge from these discussions. According to the provisions of the Gujarat Agricultural Produce Marketing Society Act, (1971) village level cooperative milk societies were required to allocate net profits in the prescribed manner. First, they have to ear-mark 25 per cent of the net profit for the reserve fund, a maximum of 12 per cent as dividend to members and a nominal amount of 2.5 per cent towards the education fund. The balance was to be distributed among members with the limit of 65 per cent towards bonus, 10 per cent as charity fund, 2 per cent towards dividend equalization fund, 5 per cent towards cooperative propaganda and 3 per cent towards research and allied activity. In addition to the above funds, an additional fund for buildings has been created by most of the societies to the extent of 25 per cent of the net profit successively. Following the above pattern it emerges the societies have accumulated a large part of their profits as reserves which are already about 500 per cent of the share capital in the Sagar and Sumul area and about 200 per cent in Sabar area. Generally, in business reserves equal to about one-third of equity are kept. It is our belief that such large reserves have been created because the final price was arrived at rather conservatively to leave relatively such large surpluses/net profits in the Sagar and Sabar area. It is, therefore, important to develop a standard in this regard. This is particularly relevant because village societies may not be required to make large capital investments other than having their own buildings. It seems that there is no necessity as such to accumulate large reserves at the village level cooperatives because even in the long run these village societies may not be required to undertake a large-scale processing activity on their own and currently such funds are used only to make term deposits.

5.3 Performance of Cooperative Milk Processing Unions

5.3.1. Coverage of the Societies

It would be relevant to point out again that village level cooperatives under the jurisdiction of processing unions in Gujarat were specialized cooperatives engaged in milk collection business. In contrast, in Maharashtra there were no primary milk societies in the selected district of Kolhapur. Two selected unions of Krishna and Warananagar in the State had linkage with the primary village multipurpose cooperative societies and the Hanuman village dairy union has yet to establish linkages at the village level in the framework of cooperatives. However, there are societies in Maharashtra Known as animal husbandry societies which are being converted now into specialized milk cooperatives.

It was observed that the selected milk processing union of Sumul in Gujarat had completed 30 years of its existence and the remaining two had completed 20 years. In Maharashtra one selected union (Krishna) had completed 20 years of its existence and the remaining two were 15 years old (Table 5.4). Despite a long historical background, selected milk processing unions in Maharashtra have yet to keep pace with the unions in Gujarat. We have already pointed out that only two unions of Krishna and Warananagar had established linkages with the village level cooperatives and another had yet to establish any linkage.

Table 5.4 : Year of Establishment and Number of Village Cooperative Societies in the Jurisdiction of Selected Milk Processing Unions in Gujarat and Maharashtra, 1976-77 to 1980-81.

State	Milk Unions	Year of Establishment	No. of village cooperatives in 1976-77	1977-78	1978-79	1979-80	1980-81
GUJARAT							
	Sumul	1951	204	259	437	581	605
	Sagar	1960	678	762	887	887	852
	Sabar	1964	616	752	825	915	1012
MAHARASHTRA							
	Krishna	1963	128	112	106	110	117
	Hanuman	1967	-	-	-	-	-
	Warananagar	1968	166	166	185	195	195

Further the number of village cooperatives linked with unions in Maharashtra was much smaller than in Gujarat. As against less than 200 village level societies in the jurisdiction of each union in Maharashtra, the number was more than 600 under each selected union in Gujarat. It may be noted that the area of operation of the unions in Maharashtra was a Revenue Block, whereas in Gujarat it was the revenue district boundary.

Apart from inter-regional differences, intra-region differences in the coverage of societies were quite marked. It was reported that generally one village unit had one society in Gujarat and, according to this norm, none of the selected unions had covered all the villages in its jurisdiction of the district. However, the maximum number of societies in 1980-81 were under the area of operation of the Sabar union (1,012 societies) and the lowest under the Sumul union (605 societies). Though the number of societies under the area of operation of Sumul and Sabar showed a steady increase during 1976-77 to 1980-81, decline was observed in respect of the Sagar union. In 1980-81, the Sagar union had linkages with 852 village societies as compared to 887 in 1979-80. An aspect emerging from the data which deserves our attention is the fact that despite a long history of cooperative milk processing, the selected unions have yet to cover villages/producers in their respective areas of operation.

5.3.2. Infrastructural Development

To provide impetus to dairy development activities and attract a larger marketable surplus of milk from the dairy farmers, the unions had undertaken several activities. Mention may be made of establishing artificial insemination (A.I.) centres, utilization of mobile vans for veterinary care, distribution of balanced cattle feed, distribution of loans to buy milch animals, etc. Provision of cattle insurance is one of the newest activity in this direction. The progress is presented in Tables 5.5. and 5.6.

(a) **Veterinary Services:** In the selected unions of both Gujarat and Maharashtra, the breed improvement programme was undertaken to increase productivity. This was done by artificial insemination of milch animals through established centres. The progress was better in Gujarat. In Gujarat, centres were established in the villages. The Sagar union had established 169 such centres for the villages covered by the union, the Sabar union 136, and the Sumul union 76. From 1976-77 to 1980-81, more than 19,000 animals were artificially inseminated by the Sagar union and about 3,000 animals by the Sabar Union. In Maharashtra, it seems this programme has yet to pick up.

As for mobile vans for animal health care, the Sagar union, on an average, treated more than 70,000 animals during 1976-77 to 1980-81 as compared to 28,000 by Sabar and about 17,000 by Sumul. In Maharashtra, lack of such facilities was observed.

Table 5.5 : Progress of Animal Husbandry and Other Services provided by the Selected Cooperative processing Unions in Gujarat, 1976-77 to 1980-81.

Dairy Union	Year	No. of A.I. Centres	No. of A.I. performed	No. of Animal cases treated by Mobile Vans	Distribution of cattle feed (metric tonne)	Supply of Lucern Seed (kgs.)
Sumul	1976-77	-	-	4870	11236	-
	1977-78	49	-	7566	15452	-
	1978-79	75	274	18906	18034	-
	1979-80	76	260	24826	22048	-
	1980-81	76	257	28663	22348	-
Sabar	1976-77	40	2000	24077	5135	10,000
	1977-78	83	1826	27799	13276	13,600
	1978-79	91	2552	29997	9048	16,000
	1979-80	122	2950	36973	11776	20,000
	1980-81	136	3576	71360	10750	9,980
Sagar	1976-77	26	1740	42419	26697	1,419
	1977-78	80	3196	49446	36808	1,493
	1978-79	105	5274	62466	31562	385
	1979-80	143	13281	91865	42668	2,399
	1980-81	169	19052	107025	43053	1,781

A.I. = Artificial Insemination

Table 5.6 : Progress of Animal Husbandry and Other Services Provided by the Selected Cooperative Processing Unions in Maharashtra, 1976-77 to 1980-81.

Dairy Union	Year	No. of Artificial Insemination performed	No. of Animals treated	No. of Cattle insured	Value of Medicines Distributed (Rs.)	Amount of Loans Distributed for the purchase of Animals	Value of cattle feed provided (Rs.)
Krishna	1976-77	528	2303	173	86191	2106550	-
	1977-78	45	2698	203	121361	109600	-
	1978-79	101	3547	74	169635	376600	-
	1979-80	2700	9940	-	212509	73400	-
	1980-81	2957	18346	-	244080	91000	-
Hanuman	1976-77	-	-	-	-	-	-
	1977-78	-	-	-	-	-	-
	1978-79	-	1550	-	-	-	-
	1979-80	50	785	-	-	-	-
	1980-81	24	540	-	-	-	-
Warananagar	1976-77	-	-	-	-	-	-
	1977-78	-	-	-	3438	-	-
	1978-79	1037	925	-	41187	-	-
	1979-80	1396	724	-	3449		-496061
	1980-81	4300	7800	-	84372		-1693184

Thus in the programme of providing artificial insemination facilities for the milch animals and treatment of animals at the farmer's doorstep in Gujarat, the Sagar union had an advantage over other selected unions. In the selected unions of Maharashtra, Krishna and Warananagar were leading in terms of providing animal care and artificial insemination facilities respectively.

(b) **Distribution of Cattle Feed:** With a view to providing cattle feed at reasonable prices, all selected unions in Gujarat had undertaken the supply through village level member cooperatives. The unions had their own cattlefeed manufacturing plants and a balanced feed was manufactured on a scientific lines. The cattle feed was sold by the union on a no-profit-no-loss basis. However, in Maharashtra, the Warananagar union had undertaken only supply of cattle feed to the members during 1979-80 and 1980-81 and had no manufacturing plant of their own. It had a contract with Hindustan Lever to meet its requirements.

The quantity of feed sold by the unions had almost doubled during period 1976-77 to 1980-81. However, viewing the requirements of cattle feed for the milch animals in the area of operation of the respective unions, balanced cattle feed supply was inadequate. The sample dairy farmers spoke about untimely and inadequate supply of cattle feed. It seems that while the disposition of the farmers towards balanced cattle feed has favourably changed more extension effort is required to increase its consumption. However, the Gujarat unions have shown substantially better results as compared to Maharashtra in this regard.

(c) **Fodder Enhancement Programme:** The Sabar and Sagar unions had also undertaken a fodder enhancement programme. Lucern seed to raise fodder on the farms of member milk suppliers was distributed. Such an activity was not promoted by any selected union in Maharashtra. However, this programme was undertaken on a preferential basis by the Sagar union due to irregular fodder availability in certain areas under the operation of the union.

(d) **Other Activities:** Distribution of loans for the purchase of milch animals was promoted by the Krishna union in Maharashtra. It seems it was logical to motivate dairy farmers in the area to supply a larger quantity of milk and accelerate dairying enterprise. However, untimely recovery of loans by the Krishna union restrained distribution of loans in 1979-80 and 1980-81 as compared to the period 1976-77 to 1978-79.

Cattle insurance is a recently introduced concept to provide dairy farmers relief from emergencies and risks. This activity was undertaken by all the selected unions in Gujarat and only the Krishna union in Maharashtra. Though detailed data on the beneficiaries of this scheme were not available, the scheme has yet to be come popular. Under the cattle insurance scheme the annual premium per cattle is equally divided between the union, the village society and the farmer.

5.3.3. Milk Collection

Adequacy and inadequacy of the infrastructural development could be assessed from the availability of milk from the societies under the area of operation of each union. Five-year data on per-society milk collection by the selected unions in Gujarat and Maharashtra are shown in Table 5.7.

On an average, per-society milk collection was about, 80,000 litres for the Sumul and Sabar unions in Gujarat. As against this quantity, the Sagar Dairy had collected double the quantity (160,000 litres). In Maharashtra, the Krishna union procured a higher quantity (105,000 litres) than the Warananagar union (65,000 litres).

The trend in per-society milk collection during the period 1976-77 to 1980-81 was quite revealing. While milk Collection in the areas of operation of the Sagar and Sabar unions showed a steady increase, in the Sumul union area, a decline was observed. An increasing trend was also observed in Maharashtra. This leads us to believe that dairy farmers in the villages seem to have accepted cooperatives as a channel for milk disposal. However, the unions will have to strive hard to keep up their confidence.

5.3.4 Utilization of Processing Capacity

Only the Krishna and Hanuman dairy unions did not have milk

processing facilities and functioned as feeder milk supplying units to the Government dairy plants. The processing facilities at Warananagar had limited handling capacity. The Sumul union had the smallest processing capacity (1.5 lakh litres per day). Sagar union has the highest processing capacity of 4.50 lakh litres per day. The Sabar union had initially small milk processing facilities of 1.75 lakh litres per day but in 1980-81 the capacity had been raised to 2.04 lakh litres per day.

Table 5.7 : Yearly Per-Village Society Milk Collection by the Selected Cooperative Processing Unions in Gujarat and Maharashtra, 1976-77 to 1980-81.

(fig. in litres)

State	Union	Years				
		1976-77	1977-78	1978-79	1979-80	1980-81
GUJARAT						
	Sumul	91,853	85,579	77,535	79,838	67,288
	Sagar	1,47,161	1,66,235	1,49,431	1,67,264	1,70,364
	Sabar	68,262	74,422	86,629	87,931	84,358
MAHARASHTRA						
	Krishna	67,059	74,933	1,04,278	1,38,705	1,41,445
	*Hanuman	14,65,725	15,49,890	17,29,407	18,47,869	14,62,869
	Warana-nagar	57,736	90,011	76,424	97,553	91,356

*Since the Union is not linked with any village level cooperative society, figures represent total quantity.

We will now examine per-day milk collection. The Sagar union continued to be leading in per-day milk procurement and increased its procurement from 2.37 lakh litres per day in 1976-77 to 3.98 lakh litres in 1980-81. Both Krishna and Warananagar unions also fared well in milk collection. But the Hanuman union could collect only about 4,000 litres a day in 1976-77 and 1980-81. However, yearly variations showed that per-day milk procurement declined in 1980-81 from the 1979-80 levels. It was reported that high prices for ghee in the open market, relatively higher milk prices available from the private trade and inability of the unions to pay higher prices were the principal reasons for a considerable drop in the supplies to cooperatives in Gujarat in 1980-81.

Milk procurement levels in 1980-81 and earlier years had their impact on utilization of the plant capacity as well. Plant capacity utilization increased in Gujarat and Maharashtra. Milk procurement

Table 5.8 : Per-Day Installed Capacity of Milk Processing, Milk Procurement and Utilization of Installed Capacity by the Selected Cooperative Processing Unions in Gujarat and Maharashtra, 1976-77 to 1980-81.

State	Dairy Union	Particulars	Year 1976-77	1977-78	1978-79	1979-80	1980-81
GUJARAT	Sumul	Installed Capacity (Litres)	150000	150000	150000	150000	150000
		Milk Procurement (Litres)	53337	60726	92832	127087	111533
		Utilization of Capacity (%)	34.2	40.5	61.9	84.7	74.4
	Sagar	Installed Capacity (Litres)	450000	450000	450000	450000	450000
		Milk Procurement (Litres)	237356	347044	363140	406474	397671
		Utilization of Capacity (%)	60.7	77.1	80.7	90.3	88.3
	Sabar	Installed Capacity (Litres)	175000	175000	200000	200000	204000
		Milk Procurement (Litres)	115208	154553	195805	220430	233870
		Utilization of Capacity (%)	65.8	88.3	97.9	110.3	114.6
MAHA-RASHTRA	Krishna	Installed Capacity (Litres)	-	-	-	-	-
		Milk Procurement (Litres)	23517	22990	30283	41789	45503
		Utilization of Capacity (%)	-	-	-	-	-
	Hanuman	Installed Capacity (Litres)	-	-	-	-	-
		Milk Procurement (Litres)	4016	4246	4738	5063	4008
		Utilization of Capacity (%)	-	-	-	-	-
	Warananagar	Installed Capacity (Litres)	100000	100000	100000	100000	100000
		Milk Procurement (Litres)	25803	40937	38736	52118	48807
		Utilization of Capacity (%)	25.8	40.9	38.7	52.1	48.8

by the Sabar union in 1979-80 was more than its rated processing capacity. However, the decline in the utilization of the rated capacity in 1980-81 as compared to 1979-80 was to the extent of 10 per cent in the Sumul union and 2 per cent in the Sagar union. It may be noted that the rated capacity of the Sabar union was increased in 1980-81 and its utilization has been more than its capacity both in 1979-80 and 1980-81. In Maharashtra, decline in 1980-81 as compared to 1979-80 in the utilization of plant capacity of Warananagar was to the extent of about 4 per cent only (Table 5.8).

The implications of the trends in milk procurement and utilization of the rated plant capacity of the selected union are that higher milk procurement has matched with the rated capacity in Gujarat and each plant has considerably improved plant utilization. But in Maharashtra, low utilization of plant capacity due to low procurement by the Warananagar union might have an impact on the economics of the enterprise. Similarly, if two other selected unions have not tried to establish processing facilities, it was perhaps due to their low per-day milk procurement.

5.3.5. Costs of Procurement, Processing and Marketing

Data provided by the balance-sheets were the only source of information for calculating handling and manufacturing costs. However, for the sake of convenience in the analysis, the costs have been grouped as follows:

(i) Fixed administrative costs :	Salaries, taxes, rents audit fees, insurance, depreciation.
(ii) Other variable costs :	Interest, stationery, postage, etc.
(iii) Raw material costs :	Cost of milk, cost of transportation, cans, acid, etc.
(iv) Manufacturing expenses :	Power, fuel, electricity repairs and maintenana

	ntenancee,processing expenses,laboratory expenses.
(v) Marketing expenses	Expenses on crates, cranes, product development, transport, stores and packing.
(vi) Dairy development expenses :	Include medicines, veterinary treatment, artificial insemination, and extension training programmes, cattle insurance, fodder development, etc.

Also various costs thus classified have been estimated on the basis of per 100 litres and are presented in Table 5.9. and 5.10.

The manufacturing activities of the unions differed considerably. The Sagar and Sabar unions had an identical product mix of milk powder, baby foods, butter and ghee whereas the Sumul union was involved only in milk pasteurization and its conversion into ghee. It may also be noted that the Sagar and Sabar unions converted more than 50 per cent of the milk into milk products while the Sumul union sold more than 80 per cent of its milk in liquid form.

On comparing the costs of procurement, processing and marketing of the identical manufacturing plants of Sabar and Sagar in Gujarat, it was observed that in 1980-81 the total cost was substantially less in the Sabar union (Rs. 294.08 per 100 litres) than in the Sagar union (Rs. 369 per 100 litres). Though the Sumul union had a different manufacturing line, the total cost of Rs. 477.14 per 100 litres in 1980-81 was the highest. The differences in the total cost were maintained throughout the period of study, i.e. from 1976-77 to 1980-81.

Table 5.9 : Costs of Raw Materials, Processing, Marketing and Other Administrative Costs of Milk Handling by the Selected Cooperative Processing Unions in Gujarat, 1976-77 to 1980-81.

(Rs. per 100 litres)

Dairy Union	Year	COSTS: Raw material costs at Union	Mfg. expenses	Fixed Administrative costs	Other variable costs	Mktg. expenses	Dairy Dev. expenses	Total
Sagar	1976-77	207.71	10.13	16.09	4.06	44.16	2.35	284.50
	1977-78	197.78	9.22	15.14	4.66	46.65	2.71	276.16
	1978-79	220.95	10.76	15.24	4.29	48.46	2.95	302.65
	1979-80	226.65	11.24	14.55	4.18	49.85	3.39	309.86
	1980-81	261.77	13.55	18.61	5.00	66.11	3.96	369.00
Sabar	1976-77	207.32	8.68	11.87	3.57	8.02	0.84	240.30
	1977-78	217.39	8.51	10.82	2.32	18.55	1.16	258.75
	1978-79	211.04	8.39	9.75	2.92	20.50	1.75	254.35
	1979-80	216.97	9.85	11.41	2.51	22.46	1.80	265.00
	1980-81	221.38	17.18	13.15	2.90	36.77	2.70	294.08
Sumul	1976-77	390.30	15.61	26.57	7.21	9.90	0.41	450.00
	1977-78	493.94	14.15	28.37	6.15	10.28	0.69	553.58
	1978-79	400.43	10.59	23.57	5.12	6.64	1.02	447.37
	1979-80	343.83	10.77	18.59	4.55	4.42	0.67	382.83
	1980-81	423.75	15.16	24.13	5.75	6.21	2.14	477.14

Table 5.10 : Costs of Raw Materials, Processing, Marketing and Other Administrative Costs of Milk Handling by the Selected Cooperative Processing Unions in Maharashtra, 1976-77 to 1980-81.

(in Rs. per 100 litres)

Dairy Union	Year	COSTS: Raw material costs at Union	Mfg. expenses	Fixed administrative costs	Other variable costs	Mktg. expenses	Dairy Dev. expenses	Total
Krishna Khore	1976-77	214.26	-	8.47	3.43	-	-	226.16
	1977-78	236.54	-	11.03	2.84	-	-	250.41
	1978-79	218.27	-	7.78	2.41	-	-	228.46
	1979-80	231.35	-	8.20	2.78	-	-	242.33
	1980-81	242.40	-	9.82	2.37	-	-	254.59
Warana nagar	1976-77	NA	NA	NA	NA	NA	NA	NA
	1977-78	219.47	7.45	15.47	14.95	7.20	-	264.53
	1978-79	223.03	9.28	17.95	12.99	7.89	-	271.10
	1979-80	224.72	9.09	14.43	12.42	12.14	-	272.80
	1980-81	257.64	12.41	16.86	13.97	16.17	-	317.05

Note : Since different items of costs pertaining to milk business were not available separately, analysis of costs for the Hanuman dairy was not attempted.
NA = Not Available

In Maharashtra, only the Waranangar union had a manufacturing line identical to that of the Sumul union. The total cost for this union in 1980-81 was Rs.317.05 per 100 litres and was substantially less than that of the Sumul union. The cost differences were maintained throughout the period of our study.

Raw material cost was the major item and it constituted between 71 and 89 per cent among the selected unions in Gujarat and between 81 and 95 per cent among the unions in Maharashtra. During the period 1976-77 to 1980-81 no large variations were noticed in the proportion of raw material cost to total cost in different unions. However, in Gujarat the proportion of raw material cost to total cost during 1976-77 to 1980-81 was the lowest in the Sagar union (between 71 and 73 per cent) as compared to the Sumul Union (between 87 and 90 per cent) and Sabar (between 75 and 86 per cent). Further, the variability over the period was the maximum in respect of the Sabar union (Tables 5.11 and 5.12) in Gujarat. In Maharashtra, yearly variations were not as large due to the fact that the proportion of raw material costs varied between 94.5 and 95.5 per cent in the Krishna union and between 81.3 and 83.0 per cent in the Waranangar union.

Table 5.11 : Relative Share of Different Items of Costs of Handling Milk Supplies by the Selected Cooperative Processing Unions in Gujarat 1976-77 to 1980-81.

(fig. in %)

		COSTS						
Dairy Union	Year	Raw material costs at Union	Mfg.expenses	Fixed administrative costs	Other variable costs	Mktg. expenses	Dairy Dev. expenses	Total
Sagar	1976-77	73.0	3.6	5.7	1.4	15.5	0.9	100.0
	1977-78	71.6	3.3	5.5	1.7	16.9	1.0	100.0
	1978-79	73.0	3.6	5.0	1.4	16.0	1.0	100.0
	1979-80	73.1	3.6	4.7	1.3	16.1	1.2	100.0
	1980-81	70.9	3.7	5.0	1.4	17.9	1.1	100.0
Sabar	1976-77	86.3	3.6	4.9	1.5	3.3	0.4	100.0
	1977-78	84.0	3.3	4.2	0.9	7.2	0.4	100.0
	1978-79	83.0	3.3	3.8	1.1	8.1	0.7	100.0
	1979-80	81.9	3.7	4.3	0.9	8.5	0.7	100.0
	1980-81	75.3	5.8	4.5	1.0	12.5	0.9	100.0
Sumul	1976-77	86.7	3.5	5.9	1.6	2.2	0.1	100.0
	1977-78	89.2	2.6	5.1	1.1	1.9	0.1	100.0
	1978-79	89.5	2.4	5.3	1.1	1.5	0.2	100.0
	1979-80	89.8	2.8	4.9	1.2	1.2	0.1	100.0
	1980-81	88.8	3.2	5.1	1.2	1.3	0.4	100.0

Table 5.12 : Relative Share of Different Items of Costs of Handling Milk Supplies by the Selected Cooperative Processing Unions in Maharashtra, 1976-77 to 1980-81.

(fig. in %)

Dairy Union	Year	COSTS Raw material costs at Plant	Mfg. expenses	Fixed administrative costs	Other variable costs	Mktg. expenses	Dairy Dev. expenses	Total
Krishna	1976-77	94.7	-	3.8	1.5	-	-	100.0
	1977-78	94.5	-	4.4	1.1	-	-	100.0
	1978-79	95.5	-	3.4	1.1	-	-	100.0
	1979-80	95.5	-	3.4	1.1	-	-	100.0
	1980-81	95.2	-	3.9	0.9	-	-	100.0
Hanuman	1976-77	-	-	-	-	-	-	-
	1977-78	-	-	-	-	-	-	-
	1978-79	-	-	-	-	-	-	-
	1979-80	-	-	-	-	-	-	-
	1980-81	-	-	-	-	-	-	-
Warananagar	1976-77	NA	NA	NA	NA	NA	NA	NA
	1977-78	83.0	2.8	5.0	5.7	2.7	-	100.0
	1978-79	82.3	3.4	6.6	4.8	2.9	-	100.0
	1979-80	82.4	3.3	5.3	4.6	4.4	-	100.0
	1980-81	81.3	3.9	5.3	4.4	5.1	-	100.0

NA = Not Available

In money value these variations in the cost of raw material were quite significant. Since the cost of raw material included the final price of milk along with the bonus and transportation, it was difficult to apportion these expenses. However, it was apparent that in Gujarat such costs in money value were the highest in the Sumul union and the lowest in the Sabar union. In 1980-81, the landed cost of milk at plant site was Rs. 423.75 per 100 litres in the Sumul union as against Rs.261.77 in the Sagar union and Rs.221.38 in the Sabar union. Variations in the landed price of milk at the union during the period 1976-77 to 1980-81 were highest in the Sagar union and lowest in the Sabar union. Raw material costs per 100 litres varied between Rs.197.78 and Rs.261.77 in the Sugar union and between Rs.207.32 and Rs.221.00 in the Sabar union. The Sumul union continued to give a much higher price for milk to their members as against the lower price paid by the Sagar and Sabar unions. However, in Maharashtra, the raw material cost at the plant site in the Krishna and Warananagar unions was low and the inter-union differences were not very large. In 1980-81, the raw material cost of the Krishna union was Rs.242.40 per 100 litres against Rs.257.64 in the Warananagar union. Also the inter-year variations in the landed cost of raw material were not very large, because per-100 litre costs of raw material varied between Rs.219 and Rs.258 in the Warananagar union and between Rs.214 and Rs.240 in the Krishna union. It must be noted that, in the first instance, the objective of the cooperative unions/village societies was primarily to find remunerative prices for the members. The Gujarat unions, therefore, adjusted the prices of milk according to revenues. However, in the case of Maharashtra, the societies operated under fixed margins and costs (including the farmer price of milk) as given to them by the Government.

It seems that transportation and related expenses on procurement are uncontrollable items in the cost structure of the unions. This is based on the fact that fixed administrative costs, other variable costs and marketing expenses constituted a very small proportion of the total costs and yearly variations were quite marginal. In the two States, an important point of difference in the component of different costs was the expenditure incurred by all three selected unions in Gujarat on dairy development. Such expenditure in the selected unions of Maharashtra was very nominal and was clubbed with other variable costs. It was interesting to note that such expenses in Gujarat accounted for about 1 per cent of the total in the Sagar and Sabar unions and less than a half per cent in the Sumul union. In money value, in 1980-81 the Sagar union Spent about Rs.4 per 100 litres of milk collected on dairy development activities against about Rs.3 by the Sabar union and Rs.2 by the Sumul union.

Among the costs other than raw material marketing costs were quite important in the Sagar and Sabar unions which had a different product manufacturing and marketing line than the Sumul union in Gujarat and the Krishna and Warananagar unions of Maharashtra. It was revealing that the marketing costs accounted for between 16 and 18 per cent of the total in the Sagar union whereas they accounted for between 3 and 13 per cent in the Sabar union. However, it is difficult to understand the reasons for such differences in costs between the two unions without an analysis of their products. Comparable data in this regard was not available. There seems to be no standardization of various costs in this regard.

5.3.6 Costs and Returns

Business activity of the selected unions in Gujarat and Maharashtra could be evaluated from the total costs and total returns accrued in the milk handling. This has been done by estimating returns on-per-100-litre basis and also of the actual amount of profit before tax accrued to them. The details for the period 1976-77 to 1980-81 of the selected unions in Gujarat and Maharashtra are provided in Tables 5.13 and 5.14.

Table 5.13 : Total Costs, Total Returns and Profits (+) or Loss (-) accrued before Tax in the Selected Cooperative Processing Unions in Gujarat, 1976-77 to 1980-81.

		Per 100 Litres (Rs.)			Actual Profit (+) or Loss (-) accrued (Rs. 000)
Dairy Union	Year	Total Costs	Total Revenue	Profit (+) or Loss (-)	
Sumul	1976-77	450.00	455.86	5.86	1096
	1977-78	553.58	560.26	7.32	1482
	1978-79	447.37	454.76	7.39	2273
	1979-80	382.83	384.76	1.93	895
	1980-81	477.14	479.27	2.13	865
Sagar	1976-77	284.50	286.30	1.80	1777
	1977-78	276.16	279.22	3.06	3278
	1978-79	302.65	304.69	2.04	2684
	1979-80	309.86	311.89	2.03	2919
	1980-81	369.00	371.83	2.83	4069
Sabar	1976-77	240.30	242.96	2.66	1118
	1977-78	258.75	262.08	3.33	1888
	1978-79	254.75	257.99	3.64	2608
	1979-80	265.00	268.74	3.74	2287
	1980-81	294.08	298.78	4.70	3992

While analysing data on costs and returns, two points deserve careful attention. In Gujarat, price realization are based on the fat content in milk and in Maharashtra price realizations till 1981 were not based on fat content. Secondly, data presented on profits before tax refer to surplus after allowing for expenditure, on account a interest charges and depreciation.

The total value of realizations accrued from milk business revealed that the performance of the Sumul union was significantly better than of the Sagar and Sabar unions in Gujarat from 1976-77 to 1978-79. In Maharashtra, total returns of the Warananagar union were higher than of the Krishna union. However, total costs did not match with total returns of the Warananagar union during the period 1976-77 to 1979-80 despite the fact that the union was engaged in processing of milk.

Table 5.14 : Total Costs, Total Returns and Profits (+) or Loss (-) Accrued before Tax in the Selected Cooperative Processing Union in Maharashtra, 1976-77 to 1980-81.

Dairy Union	Year	Per 100 Litres (Rs.) Total Costs	Total Revenue	Profit (+) or Loss (-)	Actual Profit (+) or Loss (-) accrued (Rs. 000)
Krishna	1976-77	226.16	227.01	0.85	73
	1977-78	250.41	251.16	0.75	84
	1978-79	228.46	228.95	0.49	54
	1979-80	242.33	242.77	0.44	68
	1980-81	254.59	255.04	0.45	76
Hanuman	1976-77	-	-	-	-
	1977-78	-	-	-	-
	1978-79	-	-	-	-
	1979-80	-	-	-	-
	1980-81	-	-	-	-
Warana-nagar	1976-77	NA	NA	NA	NA
	1977-78	264.53	261.94	-3.59	-537
	1978-79	271.10	265.15	-5.99	-848
	1979-80	272.80	268.45	-4.34	-827
	1980-81	317.05	319.85	+2.80	+500

NA = Not Available

Although profit was not the objective of the cooperatives, as a consequence of fluctuating costs and returns during the period 1976-77 to 1980-81, net profit per 100 litres in milk handling business also did not reveal any steady trend. This was applicable for the selected unions in Gujarat. In Maharashtra, however, profits of the Krishna union per 100 litres of milk handled declined from Rs.0.85 in 1976-77 to Rs.0.45 in 1980-81. In respect of the Warananagar union, the unit had incurred losses to the extent of between Rs.3.59 and Rs.5.99 per 100 litres during three years, 1977-78 to 1979-80, and only in 1980-81 the unit made a net profit of Rs.2.80 per 100 litres. If the latest position of per-unit profit of selected unions is examined, in 1980-81, the performance of the Sabar unit in Gujarat was the best in terms of the profit in the milk handling business to the extent of Rs.4.70 per 100 litres as compared to Rs.2.83 in the Sagar union and Rs.2.13 in the Sumul union. A profit of Rs.2.80 per 100 litres in respect of the Warananagar union in Maharashtra was comparable with the performance of the Sagar union of Gujarat. But the profits of Rs. 0.45 per 100 litres of the Krishna union were the lowest.

However,it was observed that the actual amount of net profit in the selected unions of Gujarat was quite substantial. particularly in 1980-81, the Sagar and Sabar unions earned profits to the extent of about Rs. 40 lakh each and for the Sumul union also it was about Rs. 9 lakh. The profit showed an increasing trend for the Sagar and Sabar unions. With regard to the Sumul union, increase in the actual profits was witnessed till 1978-79 and during the latter two years a substantial decrease was observed due to a fall in the total returns.

The actual amount of profit for the selected Maharashtra union was substantially lower than for the Gujarat unions. For the Krishna union profits fluctuated between Rs.68.000 and Rs.84.000 and the Warananagar union earned a profit of Rs.5 lakh only in 1980-81.

5.4 Equity-Debt Ratio

The question of sources of funds is very important in the case of cooperatives as this has a bearing on the level of participation of the members in the management decisions on the one hand and the extent and scope of operations on the other. This has been attempted for the five-year period from 1976-77 to 1980-81 and details are presented for the selected unions in Table 5.15 and 5.16. It may be noted that there was no participation of the Government in the equity capital in any of the unions. This is an important difference because in most marketing societies the Government has contributed to the share capital in a substantial measure.

Equity capital comprising share capital, reserves and other funds showed a spectacular increase in the selected unions of Gujarat. During the five-year period, equity capital more than doubled in the Sumul union and trebled in the Sabar union in 1980-81. However, increase in the equity capital in Maharashtra was very marginal. In 1980-81, the equity capital was about Rs.48 crore in the Sabar, about Rs.4 crore in Sagar and about Rs.16 crore in Sumul unions. In

Maharashtra it was Rs.25 lakh in the Krishna union and Rs. 47 lakh in the Warananagar union.

Table 5.15 : Growth of Equity and Equity-Debt Ratios of Selected Cooperative Processing Unions in Gujarat, 1976-77 to 1980-81.

Dairy Union	Year	Total Equity (Rs.000)	Index with 1976-77 =100	Total Debt (Rs.000)	Equity-Debt Ratio
Sumul	1976-77	7292	100.0	3330	69:31
	1977-78	9817	134.6	3200	75:25
	1978-79	12363	169.5	5086	71:29
	1979-80	14947	205.0	8820	63:37
	1980-81	16310	224.0	8424	66:34
Sagar	1976-77	28527	100.0	42807	40:60
	1977-78	34220	120.0	33079	51:49
	1978-79	35982	126.1	44538	45:55
	1979-80	38041	133.4	53553	42:58
	1980-81	40095	140.6	38826	51:49
Sabar	1976-77	15068	100.0	16006	48:52
	1977-78	23389	155.2	13122	64:36
	1978-79	28999	192.5	17714	62:38
	1979-80	31229	207.3	20916	60:40
	1980-81	47826	317.4	39548	55:45

One of the advantages of equity capital formation to this extent by the Gujarat union had been their relatively lesser dependence on borrowings for working capital requirements as well as investments for capacity expansion at the plant. Equity-debt ratio calculated for the purpose bears its testimony. It may be observed that the ratio of equity to debt was more than 60:40 in Sumul and fluctuated around this in the Sabar union. However, a slightly unfavourable equity ratio in regard to the Sagar and Sabar unions did not warrant any concern because these unions had embarked upon a massive programme of capacity exparsion and product diversification during 1976-77 to 1980-81.

An unfavourable equity-debt ratio was also observed in respect of the Warananagar union in Maharashtra. But the union had also undertaken several capital expansion programmes from the borrowed capital despite losses in the business and it is difficult to meet such requirements from the very low equity capital. However, it seems that the favourable equity-debt ratio in the Krishna union was on account of lack of diversification towards creation of their processing facilities.

Table 5.16 : Growth of Equity and Equity-Debt Ratios of Selected Cooperative Processing Unions in Maharashtra. 1976-77 to 1980-81.

Dairy Union	Year	Total Equity (Rs.000)	Index with 1976-77 =100 (for Krishna only)	Total Debt (Rs.000)	Equity-Debt Ratio
Krishna	1976-77	2043	100.0	381	84:16
	1977-78	1941	95.0	326	86:14
	1978-79	2168	106.1	356	86:14
	1979-80	2618	128.1	117	96:4
	1980-81	2558	125.2	265	91:9
Hanuman	1976-77	-	-	-	-
	1977-78	-	-	-	-
	1978-79	-	-	-	-
	1979-80	-	-	-	-
	1980-81	-	-	-	-
Warana-nagar	1976-77	NA	NA	NA	NA
	1977-78	2666	100.0	12324	18:82
	1978-79	2836	100.4	12369	19:81
	1979-80	4025	96.3	11873	25:75
	1980-81	4736	102.8	12665	27:73

NA = Not Available

SIX

CONCLUSIONS

6.1 Objectives of Milk Cooperatives

The milk producers' cooperatives started functioning in Gujarat in the early sixties as marketing organizations. They followed the example of **AMUL** (Anand Milk producers' Union Limited) which started in 1946 and which was also primarily a milk marketing organization. In Maharashtra, the milk cooperatives started functioning much later and the Amul pattern cooperatives began to be organized only under the Operational Flood-I Programme of the National Dairy Development Board (NDDB) started in 1969-70. Individual dairy unions in Gujarat generally defined their objectives as under:

1. Development of the cooperative milk procurement system in the milk shed area in order to provide a more remunerative channel for the disposal of raw milk to the milk producers.

2. Establishment of a milk processing-cum-manufacturing plant with a view to sell any pasteurized liquid milk and milk products particularly with a view to meeting the liquid milk demand of large urban/industrial centres.

3. Provision of technical inputs for helping farmers to increase milk production in the milk shed area, viz. cattle feed, veterinary care and animal health coverage, fodder development and artificial insemination facilities, etc.

Figure 1 : Seasonality of Milk Collection in Gujarat

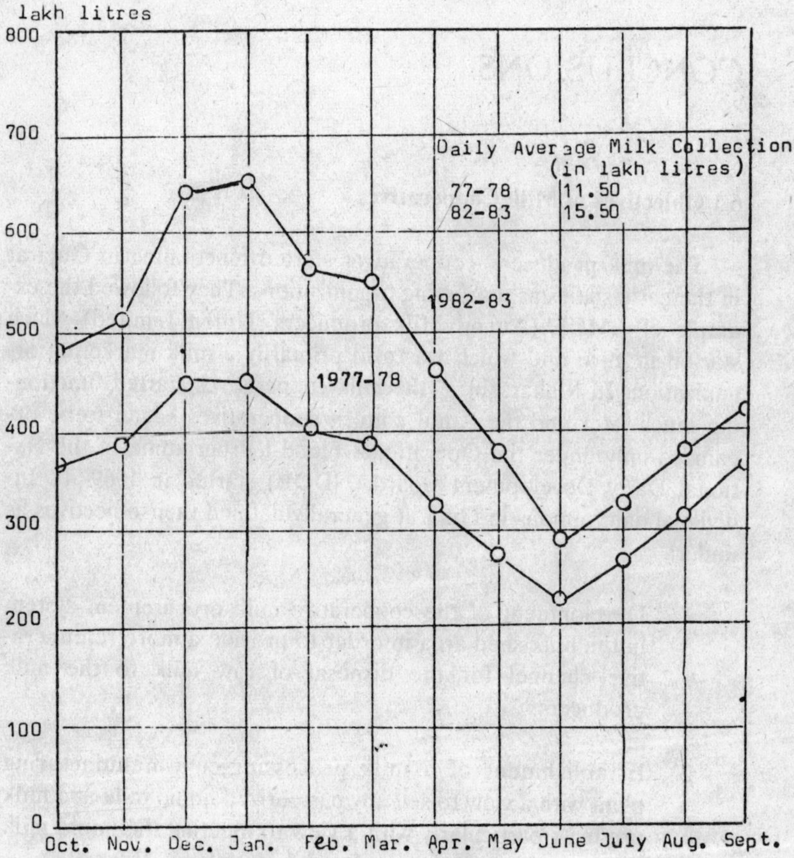

Milk collection considered for the graph plotting is of the ordinary member unions.

SEASONALITY OF MILK COLLECTION IN GUJARAT

6.2 Integration Defined

These are somewhat interlocked objectives and it is in this sense that we have called them integrated cooperatives. When a society enters marketing of members' produce and as such develops a processing, handling and distribution system under its control and ownership vertical integration can be said to be taking place. It must be noted that processing facilities are important in order to stabilize milk marketing. Milk production like most agricultural commodities not only faces seasonal fluctuations but is also highly perishable (See Figure I). Development of these facilities which which often are capital intensive requires that the organization ensures required throughputs of raw milk supplies, in order to keep the cost per unit low and enable the society to pay a remunerative price to member producers. This requires both backward and horizontal integration. Backward integration is an attempt to ensure adequate throughputs at a reasonable cost. Rather, the effort is twofold. First, that production and productivity enhancement should take place to meet the growing needs of the market and its own marketing system on the one hand and ensure on increasing income for the farmers on the other. Second, the cost of production is controlled. This is done through ownership of and control over such factors as cattle feed, artificial insemination, veterinary care and animal health facilities. Horizontal integration takes places, first, through the formation of village milk producer' societies which together form themselves into a milk producers' union which owns/ organizes the marketing system and the distribution of inputs. The village societies perform the task of collecting milk from members, and analysing each member's milk with a view to determining quality of milk for pricing as well as for bulking. It keeps records of milk supplies to the union and payment to the farmers. It also becomes an agent of the union in distributing/marketing cattle feed, provision of artificial insemination and other services. Horizontal integration thus provides an organizational mechanism whereby member producers' participation in the decision-making at different levels is ensured on the one hand and quality control, standardization of practices and use of modern inputs is ensured on the other. It can thus be noted that unless these aspects are integrated, the basic objective of assuring a remunerative price to farmers can hardly be fulfilled.

6.3 Extent of Coverage

When we designed the study we had planned to include **non-members equal to at least half of the number of members selected in each category of milk suppliers for purposes of comparison.** However, it must be admitted that in both the States in the area of the selected village milk societies it was relatively difficult to find non-members. In the case of Gujarat in any of the selected villages under the Surat Milk Producers' Union, we could not find even one non-member. In the case of the other two dairies, while there were some non-members it was indeed difficult to find them in required numbers in the selected category of suppliers. Similarly, in the case of Maharashtra we could not find any non-member dairy farmers in the big category in any of the villages under the selected dairies. It may thus be right to conclude that cooperative marketing has been internalized in these area and most farmers market most of their surplus milk through cooperatives. We have stated earlier that even the non-members in Maharashtra market about 77 per cent of their milk through the cooperatives even though private channels provided a better price. This only goes to show that cooperatives have been successful in providing a marketing channel in such areas as had none earlier or where the existing channels were inadequate. It must be noted that membership of cooperatives is voluntary and so also the decision to sell milk to cooperatives as against other channels. It needs to be noted that selected primaries and the milk unions in Gujarat were established long ago. Similarly in Maharashtra, sugar cooperatives which are well established in the selected areas were responsible for starting milk cooperatives. It would therefore, be fair to conclude that cooperatives have taken root in these areas as strong socio-economic institutions. Most of the surveyed non-members were not only uneasy in answering the question about the reason for not supplying milk to the cooperative society but often said that they were planning to become members. It appeared as if it was against the community values to be a non-member in these areas.

However, this must not be taken to mean that all the villages and all the households have been covered by the selected unions in their respective territories. Comparatively speaking, the coverage has been both more extensive and intensive in Gujarat as compared to

Maharashtra.

6.4 Characteristics of Suppliers/Members of the Cooperative Societies

6.4.1 Share of Different Categories in Total Milk Supply

It has been often argued in the case of agricultural cooperatives that they have usually served only big farmers. In the case of milk cooperatives we attempted to ascertain the share of different categories of milk producers in the total milk supplies/sales. As can be noted from the sampling plan, after having selected the primary cooperatives on each selected route, the milk collection by members was analysed with a view to selecting farmer members for the purpose of studying their milk business and the role of the cooperatives. Such an analysis showed that milk supplies ranged between 1.5 litres and 15 litres per day.

A grouping of the suppliers in the selected cooperatives revealed that milk suppliers in the small category (up to five litres per day) dominated as they formed about 38 per cent of the total suppliers in Gujarat and 51.7 per cent in Maharashtra. The medium category (5 to 10 litres per day) were the second in importance forming about 34.5 per cent in Gujarat and 22.9 per cent in Maharashtra. Thus in both States the above two categories together constituted more than 70 per cent of the suppliers. These producers on an average supplied about 50 per cent in Gujarat and about 60 per cent in Maharashtra of the total milk collection by the selected cooperatives. Notwithstanding our relative classification of small, medium and big supplier, the small and medium and big supplier, the small and medium categories in fact consisted of small producers.

6.4.2 Land Holdings of the Milk Producers

It is important to note that the volume of supply was not particularly related to the size of land holding. About 17 per cent of all the suppliers were landless in Gujarat and about 7 per cent in Maharashtra. There were 24 per cent, 16 per cent and 9 per cent suppliers in the small, medium and big categories who were landless in Gujarat. However the incidence of landless farmers was much less in the case of Maharashtra. There were only 10.5 per cent, 6.8 per cent and 10.7 per cent of the suppliers belonging to landless categories in the small, medium and large category suppliers respectively. We need to remember, however, that in the case of Maharashtra perhaps the selection of dairies in the sugar area of Kolhapur and Sangli may have caused the lower incidence due to the dominance of migrant landless labour which comes there from different parts of the State and also from other States.

It is indicative of the fact that a significant percentage of landless labourers has taken to dairy as a profitable venture in Gujarat. It may be right to conclude that the dairy cooperatives have helped them to take up dairy as a primary occupation. Further, it needs to be noted that if the usual definition of small and marginal farmer was taken into account in terms of size of land holding, then 60.7 per cent of all the member suppliers were marginal to small farmers in Maharashtra and 38.5 per cent in Gujarat. Further, they were equally important in all categories of suppliers. They formed 67.7 per cent of the small category, 64.4 per cent of the medium category and 43.1 per cent of the big category suppliers in Maharashtra. Similarly in Gujarat they formed 38.9 per cent of the small category, 39.5 per cent of the medium category and 36.8 per cent of the big category. It is interesting to note that small farmers were almost equally distributed in the small, medium and big category suppliers in Gujarat while in Maharashtra they were dominant in the small category and were also quite important in the big supplier category. If we add the landless to the small/marginal farmers then the dominance of this class becomes even more clear. In Gujarat, landless and small/marginal farmers together constituted about 53.8 per cent of the total milk suppliers while in Maharashtra they constituted 70.4 per cent of the total suppliers.

Three things need to be noted from the foregoing discussion. First, it is safe to say that the bulk of the milk supplies come from small and medium category suppliers. Second, landless labour, small and marginal farmers constitute the dominant segment of membership as well as of the supply of milk. Finally, it is heartening to note that landless labourers are taking up "dairy" as an enterprise and as a primary occupation. It can safely be concluded thus that cooperative milk producers' societies have succeeded not only in assisting small and marginal farmers but also the landless labourers and that they are indeed institutions of the weaker sections of society. We have discussed the characteristics of landless milk suppliers in the next section.

6.4.3 Landless Milk Suppliers

Earlier, it was pointed out that in Gujarat landless milk suppliers constituted about 17 per cent of the total milk suppliers. Since dairy has been looked upon as an instrument of social change and particularly because it is one of the important elements of the Integrated Rural Development Programme strategy also we have attempted further analysis of this segment in the member category.

The distribution of the landless milk suppliers in different categories is given in Table 6.1. It may be noted that amongst the medium and big suppliers there were people who owned only two or three milch animals. It is fairly obvious that such milk suppliers were selling every ounce of milk produced or else they would not be classified as medium or big suppliers. However, the large majority possessed only one to two animals and belonged to the small supplier category.

Most important, on the whole they looked after their buffaloes better. The overall wet:dry animal ratio was 64 per cent (Table 6.2.) among Landless milk suppliers as compared with the ratio of 50% observed in case of an category of dairy farmers in Gujarat (Refer Table 2.4). Further, persons having only one to two animals attempted to keep their animals wet all the time as the ratio was 100 per cent and 75 per cent respectively. This meant perhaps that they sold their dry animal after the end of the lactation and purchased a fresh animal about to come in lactation.

The milk disposal behaviour of the landless milk suppliers was no different from that of milk suppliers having land. As can be noted from Table 6.3, milk retention for domestic consumption was 14.21 per cent, 12.68 per cent and 8.14 per cent amongst the small, medium and big category suppliers respectively which was virtually in line with the general pattern in Gujarat as discussed earlier (Table 4.1). Similarly, 87 per cent of the milk was sold as liquid milk to the cooperative dairies and thus they also did not find it profitable to convert milk into ghee at home.

Table 6.1 : Distribution of Sample Landless Households in Gujarat in Different Milk Supplier Categories.

Herd size (No. of milch animals)	(members) Number of households/categories of landless milk suppliers			
	Small	Medium	Big	Total
1	10	1	-	11
2	4	5	1	10
3	5	2	1	8
4	2	1	1	4
More than 5	1	5	3	9
Total	22	14	6	42

Table 6.2 : Proportion of Animals in Milk to Total Holdings among Landless milk Suppliers of Gujarat.

Category A Landless milk Suppliers	(fig. in %) Animal in milk	Dry & Young stock	Total
Small	68	32	100
Medium	60	40	100
Big	65	35	100
Overall	64	36	100

Table 6.3 : Milk Utilization Pattern among Selected Landless milk suppliers of Gujarat (for members).

Category of Landless Milk Suppliers	Type	Domestic consumption	(fig. in %) Conversion to Ghee	Mawa	Dairy	Sales to Dudhias	Others	Total
Small	M	14.21	0.08	-	85.71	-	-	100.0
Medium	M	12.68	-	-	85.27	2.05	-	100.0
Big	M	8.14	-	-	91.86	-	-	100.0
Overall	M	11.97	0.03	-	87.22	0.78	-	100.0

M = Member

The most significant difference between the landless and other milk suppliers in different categories was in respect of the maintenance cost per animal in milk (Table 6.4). It may be noted that the paid-out cost of landless milk suppliers in the small category was only 56.5 per cent of the average small milk supplier in Gujarat. Similarly, it was 48 per cent of the medium category milk supplier. However, it was about the same in the big supplier category. The cost was less in the small and medium category because the expenditure on green fodder, oilcakes and cottonseed and medicines was much less as compared to other milk suppliers. Of these, savings in the expenditure on green and dry fodder were most significant, perhaps the landless labourer families obtained a large part of their fodder requirements in exchange for their labour on farms. It may thus be safely concluded that since the paid-out cost of such farmers is significantly lower than that of other farmers in the same category in Gujarat, particularly in the small and medium category, the economies of production have been in their favour. It is also clear that lock of agricultural land did not necessarily work as a constraint.

Table 6.4 : Maintenance Cost of per animal in milk among selected landless milk Suppliers of Gujarat (For Members Category)

(in Rs.)

Items	Category of Landless milk Suppliers			
	Small	Medium	Big	Overall
A. **Paid-out Costs**				
1. Green & dry Fodder	330	569	2258	871
2. Oilseed cakes	71	-	-	28
3. Cottonseed Concentrates	793	533	185	555
4. Gracing & Labour	98	47	-	56
5. Medium & Veterinary	175	106	34	117
6. Others	-	-	-	-
Sub-total	1467	1255	2477	1627
B. **Imputed Costs**				
1. Home Produced Fodder	687	186	74	347
2. Interest on investments of milch animals	468	455	624	499
3. Interest on Working Capital	59	50	99	65
4. Value of Family Labour	394	323	274	340
Sub-total	1608	1014	1071	1251
Total (A+B)	3075	2269	3548	2878

The difference between gross income and paid-out cost amongst the different categories of landless milk producers is given in Table 6.5. Compared to all Gujarat milk suppliers in different categories, the landless milk suppliers had the advantage to the extent of 300 per cent, 200 per cent and 73 per cent in the small, medium and big categories respectively amongst members. It may also be noted that landless farmers have a positive balance after meeting the total cost (Cost C) in all the categories while in respect of all of Gujarat all categories had a negative surplus.

On the basis of the above analysis it can be hypothesized that landless farmers exchange their labour for green and dry fodder at a great advantage. Also they are able to economize on the use of groundnut cake, cottonseed and medical expenses. While this does affect the productivity of the milch animals, it does not affect their basic economics. We may add that if they can increase their productivity, perhaps they can improve their economics of the enterprise further.

Table 6.5 : Differences in the Value of Output per Animal in Milk over Paid-out Costs, Costs A, B, and C among Landless milk Suppliers in Gujarat (for member category).

(in Rs.)

Particulars	Category of Landless milk Suppliers			
	Small	Medium	Big	Overall
1. Gross Income	3666	3828	4539	4105
2. Paid-out Costs	1467	1255	2477	1627
3. Difference in output value over paid-out costs	2199	2573	2062	2478
4. COST A	1526	1305	2576	1692
5. Difference in output value over Cost A	2140	2523	1963	2413
6. COST B	19994	1760	3200	2191
7. Difference in output value over cost B	1668	2068	1339	1914
8. COST C	3075	2269	3548	2878
9. Difference in output value over cost C	+591	+1559	+991	+1227

6.4.4 **Milch Herd Characteristics**

Qualitative Aspects

Another way of looking at the problem as to who are the beneficiaries of milk cooperative is to examine milch herd ownership. There were important differences in the herd characteristics between Gujarat and Maharashtra milk suppliers. First, the Gujarat milk producers had a preference for buffaloes which accounted for about 95 per cent of the milch animals for members and non-members. In Maharashtra, however, buffaloes accounted for only about 50 per cent of the herd. Cows accounted for the remaining 50 per cent. Thus Maharashtra had an equal preference for cows. This was so irrespective of the category to which milk suppliers belonged in both States. It is important to note, however, that a good percentage of cows owned by dairy farmers in Maharashtra were cross-breed cows purchased out of the loans advanced by the dairy cooperatives (popularly known as the Animal Husbandry Cooperatives) and guaranteed by the sugar cooperatives. As is discussed later, the Gujarat cooperatives did not encourage any such scheme nor were there sugar cooperatives to guarantee such schemes. In fact, the Gujarat cooperatives discouraged giving of loans by the dairy cooperatives at any level. Further, it must be noted that Gujarat cooperatives for a long time paid farmers on the basis of the fat content. Low yield of milk and less fat content must have discouraged farmers to keep cows. It is important to note that Mehsana and Surat districts in Gujarat, which were part of the sample areas, are known for high-yielding buffalo breeds. Thus the Gujarat over the years the farmers switched over from cows to buffaloes as a result of the presence of cooperatives. This is also evident from Table 6.6.

The other important characteristic was that in spite of the above advantage, the ratio of wet animals (animals in milk) to total milch animals was higher in Gujarat as compared to Maharashtra. It was 54 per cent in Gujarat and 50.5 per cent in Maharashtra for members. The difference was larger in the case of non-members as 65 per cent of the milch animals were wet in Gujarat as compared to only 49.5 per cent in Maharashtra. It is also important to note that the ratio did not vary between the different categories of milk suppliers.

It can thus safely be concluded that the impact of cooperative dairies in Gujarat in terms of their effort towards backward linkage to improve milk production and productivity resulted perhaps in the switchover from cows to buffaloes as their main milch animal in the first instance. Given their resource mix, it seems farmers considered it as the best strategy for optimization of their incomes from milk, However, in the case of Maharashtra, the dairy cooperatives have played but a small role in strengthening the backward linkage. Capital investment per household in milch animals in spite of the loan schemes and the presence of sugar cooperatives is much less than that in Gujarat.

Table 6.6 : Growth of Cattle and Buffaloes in Selected Districts of Gujarat.

District	Cattle (000) 1977	1972	% change	Buffaloes (000) 1977	1972	% chang
Sabarkantha	388.0	424.5	-8.6	310.6	296.7	+4.[illegible]
Mehsana	291.3	298.3	-2.2	479.9	476.6	+0.[illegible]
Surat	358.5	366.4	-2.2	133.6	120.9	+9.[illegible]

Source : Derived from **Quarterly Bulletin of Economics and Statistics, Livestock Census,** 1977, Volume 20, 1980.

Quantitative Aspects

Keeping the above facts in mind we analysed the herd size distribution over the different categories of milk suppliers. The herd size ranged between 3.12, 4.41 and 6.82 amongst member suppliers in the small, medium and big categories respectively, in Gujarat. Similarly, in Maharashtra it ranged between 2.70, 3.59 and 6.14 milch animals in the small, medium and big categories respectively. It can thus be said that the ownership of milch animals between different categories was not so skewed as in the case of other agricultural assets like land. It may also be noted that the three categories of milk suppliers in both States owned almost similar sizes of herd. However, in each category the herd size was slightly larger in Gujarat as compared to Maharashtra. Thus both qualitatively and quantitatively members of milk cooperative societies in Gujarat had a better milch herd as compared to Maharashtra.

6.5 Milk Production per Household

It was pointed out earlier that more investment in milch animals per household in Gujarat manifested itself not only in having a preference for buffaloes but also in having a larger number of milch animals per household. On an average milch animals per household were 4.05 in Gujarat as compared to 3.86 in Maharashtra. More important is the difference amongst the small category suppliers. In Gujarat this category on an average had 3.12 milch animals per household as compared to Maharashtra where there were only 2.70 animals per household. It can thus also be said that integrated cooperative dairies have helped increase investments in milch animals in Gujarat more than in Maharashtra where the cooperative dairies do not have an integrated structure. Such differences naturally get reflected in the milk production per household. Milk production per member household per year on an average was estimated at 3,178 litres for Gujarat as against only 2,719 litres in Maharashtra. More important is the fact that the average production per household on the whole was greater in Gujarat particularly because the small category households produced considerably more in Gujarat (1,545 litres) as compared to Maharashtra (1,052 litres). **Thus Gujarat small suppliers produced about 68 per cent more milk.** The above was even more true for non-members.

The medium and big category suppliers in Gujarat produced almost as much as Maharashtra medium and big category suppliers. However, it must be noted that while these two category suppliers in Maharashtra produced about equal quantity of milk per household, it was qualitatively (fat content) poorer compared to the milk of Gujarat suppliers in the same categories. As mentioned earlier, 62 per cent of the milk production of the medium category and 88 per cent of the milk production of the big category suppliers in Maharashtra consisted of cow milk.

6.6 Is Dairy a Secondary Activity?

It is usually believed that dairy is a secondary economic activity carried out by farmers which assists them to use agricultural by-products. We have already pointed out that 17 per cent of all the suppliers belonged to the landless labour class in Gujarat. Further analysis showed that 30 per cent of all the suppliers in Gujarat and 5 per cent in Maharashtra treated dairy as the primary occupation. If you add to it the fact that women usually look after the dairy operation it would be correct to conclude that marketing activities of the cooperative societies have assisted people to look at dairy as an enterprise and a primary activity. It is possible that in future as the milk production/marketing activity becomes mere profitable, more people, particularly from the landless/small/ marginal farmer class, will adopt it as a a primary occupation. It is our understanding that it is more prominent in Gujarat today because the cooperatives are older and because milk business is more profitable as compared to other alternatives.

6.7 Income and Investment

Investment in livestock was only 9.3 per cent of the total farm investment amongst the members in Gujarat and about 8.2 per cent in Maharashtra Land, housing and irrigation facilities accounted for the bulk of the investment. Milch animals represented 50 per cent of the total investment in livestock in both States. However, the proportion of income derived from livestock resources, specially milch animals, was much higher as compared to investment. For this purpose we collected data from respondents in respect of gross income from farm, labour/service and dairy sources. The results are shown in Table 6.7. It can be noted that dairy is the second most important source of income for all categories of milk suppliers. The Gujarat member milk suppliers derived 34.57 per cent of their gross income from the dairy activity while the figure in Maharashtra was 30.14 per cent. More important is the fact that dairy as a source of income increases in importance as we move from small to big milk suppliers. It is so in the case of Gujarat and less in the case of Maharashtra. However, in both cases, the proportion of income derived from this source is much higher as compared to the proportion of investment in milch herd.

6.8 Milk Costing

There have not been many studies on estimating the cost of production of milk. This is an important area where perhaps frequent and well-spread-out studies covering different centres of milk production need to be undertaken. This is so because small and marginal or landless farmers who are engaged in milk production can neither expose themselves to the risk of fluctuating market price nor to the uncertainty of disposal of milk. More importantly if milk production activity is being developed as a source of employment and income and income generation, it is important to consider the cost and price parameters. We therefore inquired into this question

Table 6.7 : Relative Share of Different Sources of Gross Income for Sample Farmers in Gujarat and Maharashtra.

(fig. in %)

Source	GUJARAT Category of milk Suppliers								MAHARASHTRA Category of milk Suppliers							
	Small farmer		Medium farmer		Big farmer		Overall		Small farmer		Medium farmer		Big farmer		Overall	
	M	NM	M	NM	M	NM	M	NM	M	NM	M	NM	M	NM	M	NM
1. Agriculture	50.66	25.61	49.15	35.78	50.89	56.65	50.83	33.50	56.73	50.37	60.30	47.90	62.87	-	60.76	
49.63																
2. Dairy	24.58	37.80	37.38	49.56	40.09	25.31	34.57	39.86	28.12	28.20	30.88	31.87	30.89	-	30.14	30.04
3. Agricultural Labour	11.68	4.84	7.48	4.28	3.24		6.76	3.96	1.83	2.23	0.59	1.11	0.46	-	0.84	1.17
4. Business	0.91	3.29	0.52	0.20	0.55	3.61	0.64	2.30	3.10	4.80	4.59	5.31	1.35	-	2.54	5.06
5. Service	12.17	28.46	5.47	10.19	5.23	14.43	7.20	20.38	10.22	14.40	3.64	13.81	4.43	-	5.72	14.10
Total	100.00	100.00	100.00	100.00	100.00	100.00	100.00	100.00	100.00	100.00	100.00	100.00	100.00	-	100.00	100.00

M = Member
NM = Non-Member

by posing in to our selected milk suppliers and non-members. Chapter III of this study discusses details in this regard. Here we will present some of the conclusions in this regard.

Our study showed that the Gujarat milk producers were able to produce milk at a lesser cost as compared to the Maharashtra producers irrespective of the category to which they belonged. Further in both States members of the cooperatives were able to produce milk at a lesser cost as compared to the non-members. We believe that the cost of production is less in all categories of milk producers in Gujarat as compared to Maharashtra because the Gujarat farmers owned buffaloes which could convert most of the farm waste/by-products into milk. On the other hand, Maharashtra farmers having more of cow milk had to spend more on green fodder and feed. This is evident from the fact that both paid-out cost and Cost C per milch animal are greater in Maharashtra as compared to Gujarat. In the paid-out cost, the component of purchased green and dry fodder and oilcakes/cottonseed or cattle feed were responsible for higher costs by about 17 per cent in Maharashtra for all categories of milk producers as compared to Gujarat. However, small producers in Maharashtra spent much more than the Gujarat farmer as compared to medium and big suppliers. It is well known that the Maharashtra dairy unions did not have their own cattlefeed plants. They sold cattle feed purchased from large producers of feed. Hence this was one reason for higher paid-out costs. Further, the fodder costs, particularly green fodder costs, were higher. On the whole it can be said that the strong backward integration aspects in Gujarat dairies such as ownership of cattlefeed plants, mobile veterinary care and other facilities may be responsible for keeping the paid-out cost at low levels as compared to Maharashtra dairies. Further, Cost C, representing imputed value of home-produced feed and fodder as well as family labour was on an average 66 per cent higher in Maharashtra than that obtained for Gujarat. If we assume that the pattern of use of family labour was not very different in the two States, it must be only green and dry fodder which can explain higher costs.

6.9 **Milk Pricing**

Members of the Gujarat dairies realized on an average Rs. 3.37

per litre in 1980-81 as against Rs.2.94 per litre realized in Maharashtra. It may be noted that each dairy settled the price of milk to be paid to the milk producer in Gujarat. There were some differences, therefore, between the unions in respect of prices paid to village societies. Two of the selected unions by and large processed most of their milk into milk products and relatively paid lower prices. The third union sold mostly liquid milk and paid relatively higher prices to the societies. However, the differences were not very large. In Maharashtra, liquid milk prices were determined by the Milk Commissioner. Further, the dairies were also required to give a percentage of their milk procurement to the Government dairy plants for distribution primarily in Bombay at fixed prices and margins. This may be the reason why Maharashtra milk producers received a lesser price as compared to Gujarat milk producers.

However, in both cases, it seemed that an attempt had been made to keep the farmers' prices at a level which would match with the variations in the consumer price index of the metropolitan cities. Given the fact that the Government plays an important role in the organization of milk cooperatives, it is not difficult to understand the above policy which is similar to the price policies followed in the case of other agricultural commodities. It is clear from our analysis of the cost of production and the price of milk realized by the farmers that the milk cooperatives in general **do not pay** remunerative prices to the producers. In fact, in real terms, member realizations have declined over the years (Table 6.8). It is difficult to understand the attitude of milk cooperatives. It is generally believed that cooperatives would increase the bargaining power of the producers. However, milk seems to be one case where the cooperatives have done nothing on this account.

We have already noted that average prices paid by the Gujarat dairy cooperatives were better than the prices obtaining in Maharashtra. Also the average prices realized by the members were better than the prices realized by the non-members in Gujarat. This is so because dairy cooperatives in Gujarat occupy a dominant position and are the real price leaders. It is for this reason that the pricing policies need to be questioned. Given the fact that the dairies are in a commanding position as far as the market is concerned, they should have attempted to obtain such prices for the members as would not only sustain their interests but would also encourage them to increase milk production and productivity. It is hard to believe that under the existing market/pricing structures, members will strive to increase production/productivity of their milch animals in any sustained manner. It is our contention that like the Maharashtra dairies, Gujarat dairies also in effect do not have the freedom to determine prices. It is well known that the bulk of Gujarat liquid milk goes to Delhi and Bombay where both procurement and consumer prices are determined by the respective Governments. Also there seem to be regulated prices for products like baby food which is one of the major products of the Gujarat dairies (Figure II). It is, therefore, suggested that if the Governments are interested in keeping the consumer prices under control with a view to protecting the interests of the weaker sections of Society in the cities, it should not be done at the cost of another weaker section living in the rural areas which has been helped by the cooperatives to take up dairying as an enterprise.

It may be noted that the cooperative dairies in Gujarat spend a considerable amount of money on cattle care, insurance, cattle feed and artificial insemination which also comes from the pockets of the farmers in-as-much as the farmers would have received that part also in terms of increased price of milk. Usually such services are provided by the Government. Further, the government gives subsidies on fertilizers to farmers to keep the cost of production of grains and other commodities under control. In the case of the dairy industry there is no such subsidy. Therefore, it is doubly important that milk prices are determined either on a cost plus basis or are left to the market forces with a support price from the Government to encourage farmers to improve production and productivity. It is only through a realistic price support that the Government can hope to make the country self-sufficient and improve the per capita milk consumption.

6.10 Nature of Gains from Integrated Cooperative Structure to Farmers/Members

We have already pointed out the differences in the structure of the cooperatives in Gujarat and Maharashtra. We intend, therefore, to use the Maharashtra cooperatives as a control group in addition to non-members for purposes of estimating gains to farmers.

Table 6.8 : Paid-out Costs and Gross Income of Different Categories of Milk Suppliers in Gujarat and Maharashtra (1980-81)

State	Category of Milk suppliers	Type of Producers	Milk Production per household (litres)	Average Sales Realization per/ltr. (Rs.)	Paid-out Cost per litre (Rs.)	Gross Income per litre (Rs.) (5-6)
1.	2.	3.	4	5.	6.	7.
GUJARAT						
	Small	M	1545	3.33	2.53	0.80
		NM	1639	3.50	3.18	0.32
	Medium	M	2765	3.45	2.23	1.22
		NM	2779	3.85	2.16	1.69
	Big	M	5980	3.33	1.54	1.79
		NM	3940	2.67	1.63	1.04
	Overall	M	3178	3.37	2.12	1.25
		NM	2110	3.41	2.31	1.10
MAHARASHTRA						
	Small	M	1052	3.49	3.28	0.21
		NM	921	3.44	3.51	0.07
	Madium	M	2836	2.90	2.70	0.20
		NM	2284	3.15	3.17	-0.02
	Big	M	6024	2.82	2.50	0.32
		NM	-	-	-	-
	Overall	M	2719	2.97	2.80	0.17
		NM	1238	2.95	3.35	-0.40

M = Member
NM = Non-Member

Monetary Gains

We have earlier analysed milk production, its cost structure and the gross income derived from milk by the producers. It may be noted that in milk production which engages a large number of landless, small and marginal farmers, the cost of production becomes very significant. It is actually what is incurred by the farmers. They influence farmers' decision in regard to the type and level of inputs to be used and the productivity/production levels to be attained. In fact, it is the nature of cash flows and the gross income which become the major factors in influencing decisions at the

Figure II : Production of Milk Products in Sagar Dairy Mehsana

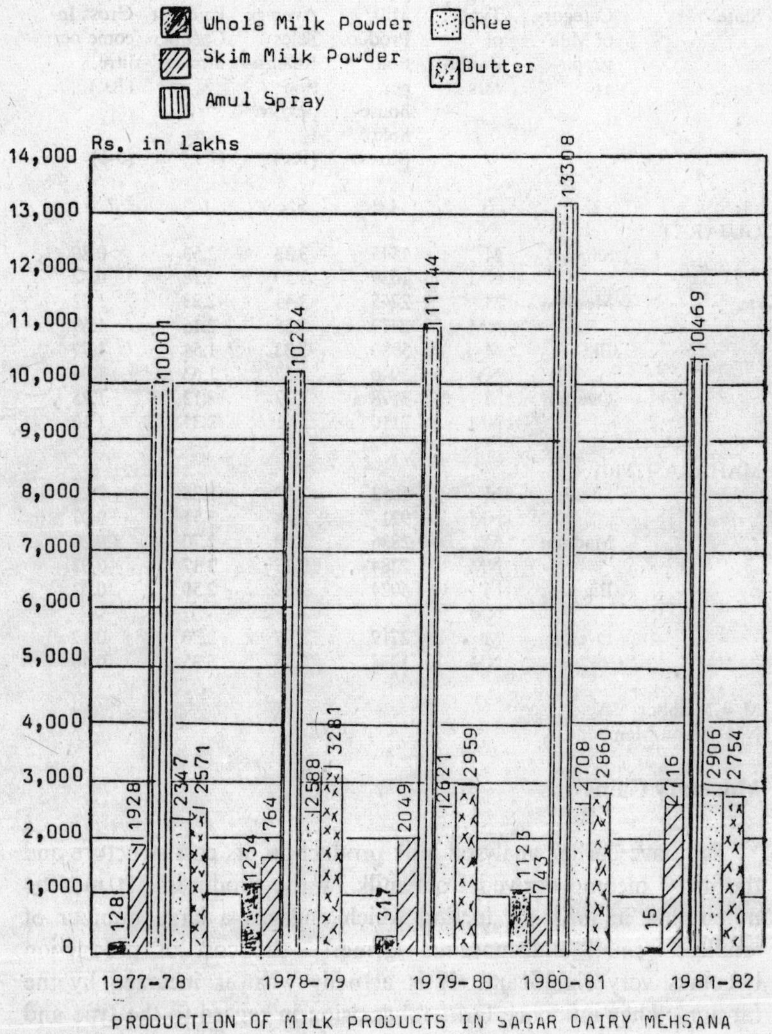

producer levels. It is significant to note that the cooperative dairies in both States have taken note of these factors and have developed a daily payment system for milk and simultaneously undertaken measures to reduce the paid-out costs.

Table 6.8 gives an analysis of the paid-out costs and gross income. It is important to note that farmers in Gujarat in all categories earn a surplus in per-litre-of-milk sales to the society after meeting the paid-out cost. This surplus increases with the increase in the size of milk sales (category of milk suppliers). Thus while the small category member suppliers have only a surplus of Re. 0.80 per litre, the big category member suppliers had a suplus of Rs.1.79 per litre. This is because the paid-out cost per litre of milk declined with increase in the quantity of milk supply. *We have already explained that this may be so because farm-produced by-products may have been used in a qreater measure by this category while in the case of small suppliers most of the inputs might have been purchased.* **This suggests that dairy business is not neutral to scale as is generally believed.**

The cooperative dairies have successfully reduced the paid-out costs. In the case of non-members in each category, paid-out costs were higher than those of the members. Most importantly, the surplus for non-members was also considerably lower in each category. The small category suppliers earned a surplus of about Rs.0.48 per litre more than the non-members. Members of all categories put together earned, however, a surplus of only Rs.0.15 more in comparison to the non-members. A similar situation prevailed in Maharashtra in respect of the gross income of members and non-members.

Based upon our understanding of the dairy cooperative structure in Gujarat, it is our conclusion that the small difference between members and non-members can be attributed to the fact that the infrastructure created by the cooperatives is quite strong and is equally used by non-members. Since cooperatives are the price leaders in the area, the non-members who supply milk to non-cooperative sources are able to get not only competitive prices but always a better price. However, this must be read with our earlier observations that a major portion of the milk production of non-members is sold to cooperatives.

The estimates of differences in the gross income between members and non-members can be below the mark because while for members' milk accounts were available from their respective cooperative societies, no such accounts were available for non-members. In both States some non-members stated that they faced problems such as non-payment on account of souring for two to three times in a month, unreliable accounts maintained by **dudhias, mawa** recovery used as an indicator of the quality of milk but which was reported to them by dudhias only). Also milk sales records in respect of prices and quantities were not available. If provision for all these facts were made, it is our belief that the gross income of the non-members could be 15 to 20 per cent less than is reported in the table. In other words, gross income of members, in comparision, may be higher.

Differences in the gross income in Gujarat and Maharashtra were more pronounced. On the whole, the Gujarat cooperatives assisted their members to net a surplus of Rs.1.08 per litre more than Maharashtra. In fact, each category of milk suppliers earned more in Gujarat. Categorywise difference was the highest for the big category where the member earned Rs.1.47 per litre more and the least for the small category where members earned Rs. 0.59 per litre more. It may also be noted that the paid-out costs are higher for each category of milk supplier in Maharashtra. Further, the differences were more pronounced for members and were substantially more in the small category suppliers. This is to be seen along with the fact that the Gujarat dairies were able to give better prices for milk to members in almost all categories. They also enabled producers to reduce paid-out costs. *Because of the combined effect of better marketing of milk due to forward integration and better supply of inputs and services due to backward integration, the Gujarat dairies were able to generate a considerably larger surplus as compared to Maharashtra* It must be noted that this is the advantage to the farmer after considerable retentions of profits by the primary cooperative and the cooperative union.

Other things remaining the same it can thus be said that the integrated cooperative structure in Gujarat on the whole assisted members to earn Rs.1.08 per litre more than Maharashtra where the cooperatives were not fully integrated.

6.11 Performance of Village Level Societies and Unions

6.11.1 Cost Structure

We have already indicated earlier that the Gujarat cooperative milk system is relatively more autonomous and more integrated than the Maharashtra system. As can be noted from Table 6.9, the Maharashtra cooperatives operated on fixed margins/costs determined by the Milk Commissioner. Amongst the three selected milk unions, Warananagar was relatively more integrated. However, it was running into losses until 1980. This is perhaps related to capacity utilization which improved from 25 per cent in 1976-77 to 48 per cent in 1979-80. Other two selected dairy unions, Krishna and Haunman, did not have a processing plant. Nevertheless, the Krishna union earned a small profit of about Rs. 0.50 per 100 litres.

Table 6.9 : Cost and Price Structure for Milk in Maharashtra (1980-81).

Particulars	Actual Rs./litre	Percentage
1. Former Price	2.97	77.55
2. Commission to Village Society (inclusive of handling cost)	0.06	1.57
3. Transport cost from Society to Union Dairy Dock	0.16	4.18
4. Commission to Union	0.06	1.57
5. Pasteurisation/processing cost	0.09	2.34
6. Transportation from Union to Bombay	0.19	4.96
7. Product manufacturing expenses (if ghee or SMP is manufactured)	0.30	7.83
Total Cost (Sale Price)	3.83	100.00

As against the above picture all the selected Gujarat milk unions had processing plants. As stated earlier, two the these specialized in manufacturing milk products (Figure II) while the third sold mostly liquid pasteurised milk. All those unions were utilizing over 70 per cent of their processing capacity. An analysis of these unions

Table 6.10 : Flow of Costs and Margins between Raw Milk Collection and Sale Value of Manufactured Milk in the Selcted Milk Unions in Gujarat, 1976-77 and 1980-81.

Particulars	Year	Sabar Amount (Rs./100 litres)	Sabar % to sale value of mfd. product	Sagar Amount (Rs./100 litres)	Sagar % to sale value of mfd. prod.	Sumul* Amount (Rs./100 litres)	Sumul* % to sale value of mfd. prod.
A. Share of Producers							
(i) Cash received	1976-77	173.61	71.5	169.54	59.2	216.18	47.5
	1980-81	213.56	71.5	200.62	54.0	232.20	48.4
(ii) Indirect benefit: Dairy Dev. Exp.	1976-77	0.84	0.3	2.35	0.8	1.02	0.2
	1980-81	2.70	0.9	3.96	1.1	2.14	0.4
(iii) Total (i+ii)	1976-77	174.45	71.8	171.89	60.0	217.20	47.7
	1980-81	216.26	72.4	204.58	55.1	234.34	48.8
B. Add Costs & Margins at Village Level Co-operatives							
(i) Costs of Handling	1976-77	3.12	1.3	1.70	0.6	3.08	0.7
	1980-81	4.03	1.3	3.36	0.9	3.46	0.7
(ii) Margins (Surplus)	1976-77	1.63	0.7	0.47	0.2	9.74	2.1
	1980-81	1.95	0.7	12.40	3.3	7.34	1.6
(iii) Total Price	1976-77	4.75	2.0	2.17	0.8	12.82	2.8
	1980-81	5.98	2.0	15.76	4.2	10.80	2.3
C. Add Costs & Margins Cooperative Milk Union							
(i) Costs of Procurement	1976-77	28.96	11.9	36.00	12.6	171.43	37.8
	1980-81	1.84	0.6	45.39	12.2	180.75	37.8
(ii) Costs of Manufacture	1976-77	8.68	3.6	10.13	3.5	10.59	2.3
	1980-81	17.18	5.8	13.55	3.6	15.16	3.2
(iii) Other costs including administration	1976-77	23.46	9.7	64.31	22.4	35.33	7.8
	1980-81	52.82	17.7	89.72	24.1	36.09	7.5
(iv) Margins	1976-77	2.66	1.0	1.80	0.7	7.39	1.6
	1980-81	4.70	1.5	2.83	0.8	2.13	0.4
D. Sale Value of Milk Manufacturing	1976-77	242.96	100.0	286.30	100.0	454.76	100.0
	1980-81	298.78	100.0	371.83	100.0	479.27	100.0

* refers to years 1978-79 and 1980-81.

revealed some very important features. Table 6.10 gives the price spread for Gujarat dairies for the years 1976-77 and 1980-81. It is quite clear that in the first instance each of the selected unions and their primaries seemed to have operated without any standard cost at any point in the milk flows from the farmer to the consumer. There are four important cost points in this flow: (i) handling cost at the primaries, (ii) transport cost from primaries to the union dairy dock, (iii) manufacturing/processing costs, and (iv) overheads of the union. There were substantial differences between the dairies particularly in respect of transport and manufacturing. Even amongst the unions having almost identical product lines (Sabar and Sagar) there were wide differences. Further, Sumul spent considerably more on transport.

While the farmer price constituted 48.82 per cent of sales realization, the cost of procurement was 38 per cent. In this manner, Sumul paid the least to farmers in relation to its sales realization, particularly owing to the high transportation cost of milk collection. It may also be noted from Table 6.10, that in spite of the fact that the Sabar union paid the highest proportion of their sales realization to farmers, they were still incurring proportionately high expenditure on dairy development activities and had the highest surplus. It is, therefore, of utmost importance to standardize costs in respect of the points mentioned earlier which alone can lead to a higher realization by the members.

6.11.2 **Capital Formation**

While comparative figures were not available for capital formation at the level of village milk societies in Maharashtra, the analysis for the Gujarat village milk societies showed that almost all societies have more than doubled their capital. In the total area of the selected unions in Gujarat, primary societies in the Sagar milk union area had the highest rate of growth in equity capital. This was followed by Sabar and Sumul. Although we have no exact data for the village societies handling milk business in Maharashtra, most of these were losing money and the societies were either stagnant or were going down in respect of capital formation.

The above is also true in respect of milk unions. The Gujarat milk unions showed a relatively higher rate of growth in equity capital as compared to the unions in Maharashtra. In fact, the Warananagar milk union was running in loss until 1979-80. There was, however, a large variation in the growth rates amongst the Gujarat unions. The Sabar union also had the highest growth rate during the period. This was followed by the Sumul and Sagar unions.

6.11.3 Dependence Upon Borrowed Capital

All the dairies over the year have expanded their activities. This invariably needs long-term capital which is often obtained from either Government sources or financial institutions. However, the lending institutions insist on a 1:2 equity-debt ratio. In the case of the selected unions in Gujarat it was much better (1:1). In the case of Warananagar which alone had a processing plant it was about 1:3. It is thus clear that the Gujarat unions are relatively more independent in this regard and usually have a better ratio as compared to the norms.

SELECTED BIBLIOGRAPHY

Apte, D.P., **Evaluation of an integrated Dairy Development Scheme (Waranangar)**, Gokhale Institute of Politics and Economics, Pune, 1982.

Bank of India, **An Evaluation of Study of Dairy Scheme for Tribals in Gujarat,** Bomabay, 1981.

Bhadure, J.Z., C.B. Singh and R.R. Patel, "Milk Production, Consumption and Marketed Surplus in some villages around Karnal", **Agricultural Marketing** Vol: 24:21, 1981.

Canara Bank, **An Evaluation study of Dairy Development Scheme in Koodaranhi, Calicut District-Kerala,** Bangalore, 1981.

Chakravarty T.K. and C.P. Reddy, "Dairy Development Programmes Process and Impact" **Journal of Rural Development,** 1982, Vol. 1, No. 1.

Dairy Industry Conference, XVII, **Special Number: Dairying in India, 1981**, Indian Dairy Association, New Delhi, 1982.

Dantwala, M.L., "Analysis of Evaluation Studies on Dairy Development Schemes", **Indian Journal of Agricultural Economics,** 1981.

Desai, D.K. and K.V. Patel, **Contribution of Dairying to Rural Economy with Special Reference to Small and Marginal Farmers,** International Dairy Congress, 1974, pp 64-75.

Dogra, B., "The White Revolution: Who gets the cream?", **The Economic Scene,** No. 7, 1981, pp. 10-19.

Food and Agricultural Organisation of the United Nations, **Detailed Report of the Second World Food Program Evaluation Mission on Operation Flood,** Indian Dairy Corporation, New Delhi, 1976.

Food and Agricultural Organisation of the United Nations, **Terminal Evaluation Report on Project India 618: Milk Marketing and Dairy Development (Operation Flood),** World Food

Program, Rome, 1981.

George, P.S. and U.K. Srivastava, "Institutional Finance for Dairy Development", **Indian Journal of Agricultural Economics,** Vol. 30, No. 3, 1975, pp. 90-6.

Government of India, **National Commission on Agriculture: Interim Report on Milk Production through Small and Marginal Farmers and Agricultural Labourers,** Vigyan Bhavan, New Delhi, 1977.

Grewal, S.S. and P.S. Rangi, "Economics of Employment of Dairying in Punjab" **Indian Journal of Agricultural Economics,** 35: p. 125, 1980, Vol 35, No. 4,pp. 120-25.

Jul, M, "Dairy Development in India: Part-I", **World Animal Review,** 1977, Vol. 24, pp. 2-8.

Jul, M, "Dairy Development in India: Part-II", **World Animal Review,** 1978, Vol. 25, pp. 30-6.

Khurody, D.N., **Dairy in India-A Review,** Asia Publishing House, Bombay, 1974.

Nair, K.N., "Technological Change in Milk production: A Review of Some Critical Issues with Reference to South Asia", **Economic and Political Weekly,** 1982, Vol 17, No. 13, pp. A15-20.

Nyholm, K.H., Schaumburg-Muller and K. Westergaard, **Report on Livestock (Dairy) Development in the Bangalore Milk Shed Area,** Institute for Development Research, Copenhagen, 1975.

Nylom, Klans, H. Schaumburg-Muller and K. Westergaad, "Socio-economic Aspects of Dairy Development", **Economic and Political Weekly,** 1974, Vol. 19, No.52, pp A-127-35.

Patel, A.S. and Jodha N.S., **Economic Relationship between Crop Farming and Dairying in a Developing Area: A PL 480 Micro Level Study of South Gujarat,** Sardar Patel University, Vallabh Vidyanagar, 1979.

Patel, S.M., D.S. Thakur and M.K. Pandey **Impact of the Milk Cooperatives in Gujarat,** Institute of Cooperative Management, Ahmedabad, 1975.

Patel, S.M., and Pandey M.K., **Economic Impacts of Kaira District Cooperative Milk Producers Union (Amul Dairy) in Rural Areas of Kaira District (Gujarat State),** Institute of Cooperative Management, Ahmedabad, 1976.

Patel, V.C. and M.D. Desai, **Factors Affecting Milk Supply to Cooperative Dairies in Gujarat: A Study of Amul and Dudhsagar Dairies,** Research Study No. 46, Sardar patel

University, Vallabh Vidyanagar, 1976.

Pichholiya, K.R., "Bovine Economy of Panchmahals District : A Study", **Indian Journal of Agricultural Economics,** 1975, 30:3, p. 141

Sambrani, S., **Transforming the Rural Poor : The Big Push in Action (The experience of Operation Flood),** Institute of Rural Management, Anand, 1980.

Setty, Rajappa, "Karnataka Dairy Development Project : A Profile of Performance", **Southern Economist,** Vol. 19, p. 57-58.

Shah, Dilip, "An Estimate of Employment and Income Benefits Generated by Amul Dairy," **Anvesak,** Vol.11, 1981, pp 281-301.

Shah, Dilip, "An Economic Analysis of Baroda City Milk Price Problem", **Vishleshan** (1981), No. 7, pp. 43-45.

Shah, D., "Dairy Development Strategy–An Assessment", **Kurukshetra,** 1981, Vol. 29:7, pp. 8-18.

Shah, M.M., **Integration of District Dairy Cooperatives in Gujarat,** Sardar Patel University, Vallabh Vidyanagar, 1977.

Singh, S.P. and P.L. Kelley,**Amul: An Experiment in Rural Economic Development,** Macmillan India Ltd., New Delhi, 1981.

Somjee, A.H., and G. Somjee, Cooperative Dairying and the Profiles of Social Changes in India", **Economic Development and Culture Change,** 1978, Vol 26:3, pp. 577-597.

Thakur, D.S., "Impact of Dairy Development Through Milk Cooperatives : A Case Study of Gujarat", **Indian Journal of Agricultural Economics,** 1975, Vol 31:3, pp. 83-89.

Thakur, D.S., "Milk Co-operatives in Gujarat : The gainers are small farmers, landless", **The Economic Times,** April 25, 1977.

Union Bank of India, **Dairy Development in Nasirabad,** (Jalgaon), Bombay, 1982.

INDEX